The Emmanuel Factor

The EMMANUEL FACTOR

Nelson L. Price

BROADMAN PRESS
Nashville, Tennessee

© Copyright 1987 • Broadman Press
All rights reserved
4250-50
ISBN: 0-8054-5050-5

Dewey Decimal Classification: 248.4
Subject Headings: CHRISTIAN LIFE // SPIRITUAL LIFE
Library of Congress Catalog Number: 87-9317
Printed in the United States of America

The Scripture quotations in this book are
from the *New King James Version*. Copyright
© 1979, 1980, 1982, Thomas Nelson, Inc.,
Publishers. Used by permission.

Library of Congress Cataloging-in-Publication Data

Price, Nelson L.
  The Emmanuel factor.

  1. Jesus Christ—Significance—Meditations.
I. Title.
BT304.7.P75 1987   231.7   87-9317
ISBN 0-8054-5050-5

Dedication

To My Brothers and Sisters
in Christ
in whom
I have seen
The Emmanuel Factor effective

Contents

1

God with Us in *History*

Part I

Dawn was not fully awake. Life was only beginning to stir in the listless German prisoner-of-war camp. Despair made every dawn unwelcomed.

Dr. Murdo Ewin MacDonald, a Scottish Presbyterian, was slow to respond to the whispered appeals of an American friend to awaken. Once aroused he grew intently interested and responded to encouragement to come aside and hear good news brought by another Scotsman. His friend had secretly been listening to the BBC. Good news had been received of the allied invasion of Normandy. The bearer of the good news whispered only three words in Gaelic . . . "They have come."

MacDonald threw reserve and restraint aside, ran back into the barracks, and began shouting: "They have come. They have come." Response was instant and incredible. Weak men shouted as they jumped for joy. Rugged men hugged each other and wept with glee. Some stood on tables and shouted as others rolled on the floor in fits of elation.

Their German captors, not knowing of the D-Day

invasion, thought them crazy. The jubilant allies were still prisoners within the formerly intimidating walls. Nothing had changed outwardly. Inwardly they knew everything had changed.

Dateline Nazareth:

Nazareth! A teenage girl was on her regular, routine trip to the city well for water. This unsophisticated, innocent girl became only the second person to see an angel in over 400 years. Imagine her amazement! The angel spoke: "Rejoice, highly favored one, the Lord is with you . . ." (Luke 1:28). That was the first vibration on heaven's harp announcing God would soon be with us all.

Her open-mouthed puzzlement being observed, the angel spoke again, "Do not be afraid, Mary, for you have found favor with God." She was the first to know that which the world was soon to realize. God not only is not angry with us, but He actually loves us.

Again perceptive of her quizzical look, the angel explained how the miracle of her conception would be possible in her virgin state: "For with God nothing will be impossible" (Luke 1:37).

Then exuded Mary, "Let it be . . ."

Nine months lapsed.

Dateline Bethlehem:

Bethlehem! Long lay the world in sin and error pining. This little town, itself cradled in obscurity, was anesthetized by hopelessness. The city slumbered in sin's stupor. Humankind was captive.

Then came the good news delivered by angels: "There is born to you this day in the city of David a Savior, who is Christ the Lord" (Luke 2:11).

A band of angels joined that herald in praising God by saying, "Glory to God in the highest, And on earth peace, good will to men" (Luke 2:14).

Then all heaven broke out.

The Ancient of Days became a newborn one night in Judea.

Mary had a little Lamb who was the Lion of the Tribe of Judah.

A dark night's sky formed a canopy for the Light of the World.

The Fountain of Life nursed at a blessed woman's breast.

Before His brief earth walk would end, He would leave the footprints of God in the Judean sands and stain the grey stones of Calvary with God's red blood.

Matthew reminded the era that Isaiah (7:14) had prophesied of this One, ". . . they shall call his name Emmanuel, which being interpreted is God with us" (Matt. 1:23).

Today you can visit the historical spot of Christ's birth in a well-preserved cave in Bethlehem. Every time I visit there I pause to marvel and reflect that here, right here, "The Word became flesh and dwelt among us . . ."

The Emmanuel Factor was now at work.

The Greek participle "with" means "together with" or "sharing with" us. It speaks of a close fellowship. In His birth Jesus entered into our sphere. No longer could man speak of the remote indifference of heaven. God was now at work with His sleeves rolled up, involved in getting His hands dirty purifying our souls.

Let heaven and earth rejoice! Freedom is now available to captive humankind. We too should revel and rejoice as we go about living in our new freedom.

All of humankind since the day of Adam and Eve have been born in the slave market of sin. All have been held captive by the concentric walls of our old sin nature and our personal sins. In order to free us, it had to be done from within the compound of prisoners— humanity. One would have to be born within the compound in order to provide a way out. However, if one were born within the incarcerating walls of the old sin nature and personal sin that one, too, would be bound by the same restraints as all captives. Therefore, a miracle was necessary. One had to be born without the limitations of the old sin nature. Then, while still in the human form, this one would have to live without one single personal sin. Only then could this one exit and liberate whoever would follow Him. For one to be so born, a miraculous conception by a virgin would be necessary. Since this never had happened, it was thought to be impossible. Since it never happened again, that causes many still to think it inconceivable that a virgin could conceive. Simply because it is a unique phenomenon, it is considered by some to be impossible. Enter God!

The result—a miraculous rescue.

Once on a flight my seat companion was the chief labor mediator for the president of the United States. He did not know my identity, so the answer to my question was not tainted when I asked his definition of a "mediator." He explained that a mediator has to be equal to both parties in order to represent both properly. That is still the most profound definition of a mediator of which I know. It did not come from a book of theology, or from a seminary class, but it is unexcelled. In light of this definition 1 Timothy 2:5 is better understood: "For there is one God, and one Mediator between God and men, the Man Christ Jesus . . ."

He and He alone, the God/man-man/God, is equal to both God and man; fully God and wholly man. God the Son who is co-equal, co-essential, and co-eternal with God the Father (John 1:14,18) entered into the sin-bound prison camp as the free God/man-man/God to free captive humankind.

THE DIVINE NATURE

Jesus Christ, "who, being in the form of God, did not consider it robbery to be equal with God . . ."

The writer of Hebrews (10:5) reminded his readers that the Psalmist (40:6-8) had forespoken of Emmanuel's form: "a body you have prepared for Me."

In a virgin womb the Holy Spirit bypassed the process of impregnation and made fertile a heaven-designed embryo. Thus, the virgin Mary conceived.

Christ's comment, regarding another matter considered by persons of His day to be impossible, is applicable: "With men this is impossible, but with God all things are possible . . ." (Matt. 19:26).

The God of this universe, Who made the laws of nature as a protection and guideline for us, did not make them as a strait jacket for Himself. A miracle by its nature is an alteration of the norm. To believe a miracle is to accept supernatural intervention. The virgin birth introduced a new era in the course of the universe. It is explainable only by the true entrance of the creative power of God in sharp distinction with the order of nature. This phenomenon is no meaningless freak of nature but an organic part of God's mighty redeeming work. To accept the virgin birth is to take the momentous step of affirming the entrance of the supernatural into the realm of the natural.

Satan has under perpetual assault the reality of the virgin birth. He knows that to deny it is to reject the authority of Scripture. To deny it is to refute the supernatural in connection with our beloved Lord. It also leaves humankind in the slavemarket of sin with no way out. Thus, three major doctrines live or die with the virgin birth: the inspiration of scripture, the Deity of Jesus Christ, and the redemption of humankind.

The virgin birth was patently the method used by

God the Creator Who formed the first Adam to prepare a body for the second Adam, Jesus Christ. To concede God's existence is to admit the potential of the virgin birth.

My friend, Claude Brown, founder and owner of Brown Trucking Company, shared the following with me. His company has offices in approximately 150 cities across America. In considering a person for employment a polygraph test is given. The operator of his "lie-detecting" device has provided him with a sworn affidavit regarding one part of the test given every would-be employee. The operator asks, "Do you believe there is a God?" In every instance when a professing atheist has answered "no," the test has shown the person to be lying.

A quote from NASA pioneer, Dr. Werner von Braun, speaks to the obvious evidences of God's existence: "The public has a deep respect for the amazing scientific advances made within our lifetime. There is admiration for the scientific process of observation, experimentation, or testing every concept to measure its validity. But it still bothers some people that we cannot prove scientifically that God exists. Must we lift a candle to see the sun?"

To accept the premise of God makes accepting the potential of the virgin birth easy. He who spoke the universe into existence could surely have made the entrance of His virgin-born Son into the slave market of sin possible.

Before Bethlehem, God's Normandy, Jesus Christ had existed in eternity as Deity. Paul spoke great truth to young Timothy when he wrote: "great is the mystery of godliness: God was manifested in the flesh . . ." (1 Timothy 3:16).

John wrote (1:1), "In the beginning was the Word, and the Word was with God, and the Word was God." His reference was to Jesus Christ.

The Greek text literally means "before time began to begin." In considering creation we usually think of the emergence of the universe. However, John informs us that time itself was a part of creation. Our universe, principally our planet, is time-locked. However, before the evening and the morning were the first day, Jesus Christ existed in eternity.

John was discreet in choosing a name for Christ in this text. He used the Greek word *logos*, which is translated "Word." To understand the meaning of a word it is wise to see how it is used. Plato had previously used *logos* as a term meaning "all that is known or knowable about God." Thus, Jesus is all that is known or knowable about God.

He "was God" and "was with God." Superficially, these two statements seem to be in contradiction. Actually they are complementary.

Jesus "was God" in essence. That is, all that God the Father was, God the Son was. The Father was holy, righteous, just, eternal, unchanging, all-powerful, and all-knowing. So was the Son.

Jesus was existing "with God" in eternity past. There never was a time when God the Son was not and was not with God the Father. Christ existed in eternity as a member of the Holy Trinity: God the Father, God the Son, and God the Holy Spirit. They being three persons are one in essence, that is, nature.

H_2O exists in three forms. As a liquid it is water. When frozen it exists as a solid, ice; and when boiled it exists as a gas, steam. Water is three in one, and in each state it has the same essence, nature.

Christ is spoken of as "being in the form of God" (Phil. 2:6). "Being" translates the Greek *huparchein* which is used to refer to the innate, unchangeable, unalterable characteristics and abilities of a person. This term reveals Jesus always was God, was with God, and still is God for and with us.

"Form" translates the Greek word *morphe*, meaning essence or nature. In nature or essence He was God. Our human form, our *morphe*, is *homo sapiens*. It doesn't change.

Christ was, as His name Emmanuel signifies, "God with us."

The elders at Ephesus received this insight: "Therefore take heed to yourselves, and to all the flock, among which the Holy Spirit has made you overseers, to shepherd the church of God which He purchased with His own blood" (Acts 20:28). "He" refers to God. God is here identified as being Christ in that it was His church "purchased with His own blood."

Roman Christians were informed that "Christ came, who is over all, the eternally blessed God" (Rom. 9:5).

Timothy was left with no doubt about Christ's being God when Paul instructed him, "God was manifested in the flesh" (1 Tim. 3:16).

Titus was exhorted to keep "looking for the blessed hope and glorious appearing of our great God and Savior Jesus Christ, who gave Himself for us, that He might redeem us from every lawless deed and purify for Himself His own special people, zealous for good works" (Titus 2:13-14). Jesus is here represented as God who came to rescue us from the slave market of sin.

The writer of Hebrews spoke of God the Father as designating Jesus, God the Son, as the one ". . . whom He has appointed heir of all things, through whom also He made the worlds; who being the brightness of His glory and the express image of His person, and upholding all things by the word of His power, when He had by Himself purged our sins, sat down at the right hand of the Majesty on high . . ." (Heb. 1:2-3).

Herein, Christ is again depicted as the One liberating repentant sinners from the slave market of sin. As a result of the faithful and successful work of Jesus, God the Father declared, "Your throne, O God, is forever and ever . . ." (Heb. 1:8). Here God the Father refers to Jesus as "God."

With confidence born out of supernatural insight, John closed his first epistle on a note of assurance:

> And we know that the Son of God has come and has given us an understanding, that we may know Him who is true; and we are in Him who

is true, in His Son Jesus Christ. This is the true
God and eternal life" (1 John 5:20).

Throughout much of this letter John has been expos-
ing idols and spurious gods. In this verse he represents
Jesus as having come to reveal God the Father as the true
God. Jesus' mission was to enable us to "know Him who
is true." John immediately turns the truth to face in the
other direction and uses "This" as a reference to Jesus. Of
"This" one it is written, "He is the true God and eternal
life." Our faith-life hangs on the hinge of His Deity. As
God the Father is made known to us by Jesus as "Him
who is true," so also the Father's Son is made known to us
as "the true God." This one, "His Son Jesus Christ," is the
true God!

HIS HUMAN NATURE

In Philippians 2:6 the inspired penman used the
Greek word *morphe*, translated "form," to refer to
Christ's Deity. In that same chapter, in verse 8, He uses
the Greek word, *schema*, translated "appearance," to refer to His human embodiment. As human beings our
schema takes on different appearances. One is that of an
infant; then we move through such stages as adolescence,
teen years, young adult, middle age, and senior adult. In
each stage our outward form changes, but our nature remains the same—*Homo sapiens*.

In Bethlehem, Jesus, whose eternal form *(morphe)*

was that of Deity, willingly took on the outward appearance *(schema)* of a human being. Though a man, He was still God.

Modeling clay may be shaped like a cube at one point. Carefully it can be reshaped into a ball. This causes its appearance to change—but not its nature. When Jesus stepped through the portal of heaven and across the threshold of earth His appearance changed, but not His nature. He became man who was and is God.

This is called the *kenosis,* self-emptying of Christ. He gave us a living illustration of taking on the form of a servant. At the Last Supper, He took off His outer garment, illustrating He had laid aside His Deity for personal use. By girding Himself with a towel He was illustrating that He had taken the form of a servant. The towel in that era symbolized servanthood. In kneeling before His disciples, His inferiors, He demonstrated His humility.

We should each join "The Royal Order of the Towel" and become His servant.

A recent eighteen-year-long study concluded that all high achievers share three things in common: (1) a sense of mission, (2) ability to set goals, and (3) and confidence. Jesus manifested all three. His sense of mission was summarily stated as: "I have come that they might have life, and that they might have it more abundantly" (John 10:10). His ability to set goals is found in His declaration: "[I have] come to seek and to save . . ." (Luke 19:10). His confidence, though often revealed, is best illustrated by taking the towel and showing He could control Himself.

Jesus was the optimum form of God and the ultimate form of man.

Gospel writers take great pains to give emphasis to Christ's humanity, as well as His Deity. Remember, a mediator has to be equal to both parties. Therefore, if He is going to reconcile God and man, He must be equal to both. Only by the virgin birth could He enter the slave market of sin to set the captive free. In order to liberate sin-enslaved man, He had to be enslaved, though free from sin. His virgin birth freed Him from inherent sin, that is, the old sin nature. His being of the seed of woman made Him vulnerable to the potential of personal sin. Living without one single personal sin He was thus free from its penalty. His advent in the City of David put Him in position to save lost humankind.

Jews have always tenaciously valued their pedigrees. This is one method the Father used to let us know which one of those born of the seed of woman was "the" One who would redeem us. Prophetically, God the Father had very narrowly defined the conditions of the birth of Jesus. Through a long history the Father had revealed such insights as His descent from Abraham (Gen. 12:3), His tribe being that of Judah (Gen. 49:10), His lineage that of David (Isa. 9:7), the place of His birth as Bethlehem (Mic. 5:2), the time of His birth (Dan. 9:25), His virgin conception (Isa. 7:14), the slaughter of innocent children in conjunction with His birth (Jer. 31:15), and the flight into Egypt (Hos. 11:1).

Supported by such a well-known pedigree, Matthew, a tax collector, and Luke, a medical doctor, wrote.

Matthew, writing to a Jewish audience, initially presented Jesus as the King and Messiah descending from Abraham through David to Joseph.

Luke started with Jesus and traced His lineage back through Mary to Adam. Matthew ends with Jesus, and Luke begins with Him. This is an indirect way of saying, "Anyway you look at this, Jesus is the One promised."

Matthew shows the legal royal line.

Luke shows the lineal bloodline.

The royal line was always passed through the father. The father had the right to rule. Jesus had no natural father. When Joseph married Mary he became Jesus' legal father. Marriage involved automatic adoption. The adopted child had all the rights of the adopting father. Thus, through Joseph's lineage He had the right to rule.

Mary was a descendant of one of David's sons, Nathan. In this way, through Mary, He had the bloodline of David.

By the miraculous virgin birth, the Father also resolved another seemingly insoluable complexity. Jeremiah 22:30 records the story of Jeconiah against whom a curse had been placed forbidding any of his descendants from ruling on the throne of David. Joseph was a descendant of Jeconiah. If Jesus had been the natural-born son of Joseph, He could not have been the One prophetically spoken of as ruling on the throne of David. God the Father devised the virgin birth as the means by which

Jesus could descend from Jeconiah without being under the curse.

At the time of Jesus' birth and during His life the Temple stood in Jerusalem. It served as a sort of courthouse in which all family records were kept. In this way Jews could trace their genealogy. Jesus' role as the One to liberate sinful man was never contested from a pedigree standpoint. The records were there at the time to validate it.

According to Numbers 26 and 35, after the conquest of Canaan all persons had to be able to validate their tribe, family line, and father's house. This was essential in order to legally identify the proper location of their inherited land.

Ruth 3 and 4 indicates that land could only be bought or sold within one's own tribe. One's genealogy was essential for commerce.

Those records were destroyed when the Romans pillaged Jerusalem in AD 70. They are no longer available. If Jesus were not the One promised by the Father as the One to free us from sin, there is now no way to validate anyone who pretends to be the Liberator. If Jesus were not the One, it is now too late for prophecy to be confirmed. This is all the more reason to know He was the ONE.

Little details often verify a truth. In Cobb County, Georgia, law-enforcement authorities tracked a plane by radio from the moment if took off in Bogota, Colombia. Its cargo of cocaine was valued in the millions of dollars.

Upon landing the crew was arrested, the plane and cargo impounded. On board was a piece of wood with a peculiar-looking worm crawling out of it.

As a part of the defense the lawyers contended that the plane had never been to Colombia. False records seemed to confirm this. As the last bit of evidence the prosecution presented the worm. They had sent it to Arizona to be identified by one of the nation's foremost entomologists. He certified that it was a rare worm found only in the forests near Bogota. Conviction consequented from a simple certified truth.

Over 300 prophecies preceded the birth of Christ. Every one is a "worm" attesting His Deity. An analogy has been drawn of the unlikelihood of all these coming true in one life. It would be as unlikely as a man finding a certain silver dollar under these conditions. If silver dollars were stacked knee deep over a land mass the size of the state of Texas and one marked with an "X," a man blindfolded at midnight would have a better chance of finding that dollar in one hour than all the prophecies regarding Christ coming true by accident.

Paul wrote the church at Rome "concerning His Son Jesus Christ our Lord, who was born of the seed of David according to the flesh, and declared to be the Son of God with power, according to the Spirit of holiness, by the resurrection from the dead" (Rom. 1:3,4). The participle "was born [made]" means He came into being. The verb "to be" in essence means He always had been. There never was a time when He wasn't the Son of God.

"Son" isn't used in the sense of offspring, but associ-

ation. A big unabridged dictionary will give this definition of "son": "a male person looked upon as the product
or result of particular agencies, forces, influences, etc.;
'sons of liberty'; one associated with." "Son" as applied to
God the Father and Son has nothing to do with prodigy
but association. James and John were called "the sons of
thunder" (Mark 3:7). The name Barnabas meant "son of
encouragement" to show his identity with encouragement. Son as used of Jesus speaks of association, not generation. It was His unique title identifying Him as Deity.

From British history comes an account which illustrates His reason for coming to earth.

The Duke of Norfolk was a loyal and loving subject
of his esteemed king. As a gesture of friendship he gave
the king a priceless Portland vase. It was so highly treasured by the king that he had it placed in the British Museum. In this way he could share it with all the kingdom.

A household servant of the Duke of Norfolk became
envious of him and sought to kill him in order to steal his
estate. Finding this out the Duke banished him. Smol-
dering with envy, bitterness, and rage the servant sought
revenge. He chose the Portland vase as the channel for his
viciousness.

Going to London he visited the museum. For days
he studied the routine of the guards. At a predetermined
time, when the guards were being changed and no visi-
tors were in sight, he stepped across the restraining cord
and seized the vase. Checking to see that he was unob-
served he raised the vase over his head and, with all of his
might, dashed it on the floor. It broke into innumerable

small pieces. The priceless treasure was ruined, broken. Or, so it seemed.

The king ordered all the pieces saved. A search was made for someone who could restore the vase. At last a descendant of the maker of the vase was found who possessed such skills. For weeks he labored until at last it was restored. Only close examination could detect it had ever been broken. Today this same vase can be viewed in the British Museum in its restored glory.

Lucifer, an archangel, served the throne of God. He sought to lead an insurrection against God and establish his throne above that of the Most High God. As a result he was banished from heaven. Seeking revenge he came to earth and craftily broke humankind's relationship with the Lord. God desired for this broken relationship to be restored. In coming to earth, Jesus was on a mission. He was to put the pieces back together.

Literally, His role was to bring God and mankind together. By being born in the slave market of sin He was in position to set the captive free. He overcame the barrier of our old sin nature by being born of the virgin and having no such nature. It is for this reason we can rejoice that infants who die are at home with the Father. They have no personal sins, and Christ died for our sin nature. Therefore, they are set free.

We, with our personal sins, still need a deliverer. He lived without one single personal sin and thus was the fitting substitute in payment for our personal sins. There is a breach in the concentric sin barriers. It is the person Jesus Christ who came to set the captive free. The issue now is: Who will follow Him in faith to eternal freedom?

"God was in Christ reconciling the world unto Himself . . ." (2 Cor. 5:19). God was not in Christ in the sense that He was simply using Him, but through the unique union of the incarnation He was Christ.

"Your iniquities have separated you from your God" (Isa. 59:2). This elemental realization enables an awakening to the need for liberation from sin's compound. Often the sin barrier is so attractive that persons fail to realize its effect—separation.

The world at the time of Christ's coming was in a position depicted by an altar in the great cathedral at Marizell, Austria. At the foot of a cross is a large silver globe. All continents are seen in outline on it. The unique feature is a serpent encircling the earth. It depicts the world as being in the grip of sin. That was the dilemma when Emmanuel arrived on the stage of history.

In this compound *The Emmanual Factor* was the only hope. "For He Himself is our peace, who has made both one, and has broken down the middle wall of division between us" (Eph. 2:14). There is a breach in the barrier. The passage through it is marked by a cross and an open, empty tomb.

In Nazi prison camps—defeat, despair, and despondency permeated all of life. A sense of hopelessness prevailed. A French doctor coined a word for this condition. He called it "barbed-wire sickness." A principal symptom was an appalling sense of futility and meaninglessness. No matter what activities were planned nothing could cause the prisoners to forget the barbed wire. Despair and emptiness were as much their captors as the Germans who stood guard over them.

That same condition prevails today in lives apart from Christ. The barbed wire has separated us from God and isolated us from one another. Without Christ persons are preoccupied with the barrier of separation—sin.

There is a heavenly-devised plan to enable the captives to be set free. Paul said it was God "who reconciled us to Himself through Christ" (2 Cor. 5:18).

The word "reconciled" translates the Greek *katallaxantos,* which means "change completely." God's purpose is to change relationships with Him completely by removing the sin barrier at Calvary.

In another country in another day an abandoned infant was found. The finder took it to a foster care home. People there assuming it to have been conceived out of wedlock refused it, saying it was the product of sin and destined by God to die. The would-be rescuer said, "When God wished someone to die for sin He sent His Son."

That is how He opened the slave market of sin to set the prisoner free. Life is made possible by death. He died that we might live. His death provided our ransom.

Now that we know God is with us from an historical perspective our rejoicing should be no less great than those in the German POW camp when they heard of their impending rescue. Ours is no less certain. He has come! He has come! Few things change externally because of this fact. Everything changes internally because it is a fact.

This results in joy to the world. This joy isn't a bonfire-pep-rally kind of energy-of-the-flesh elation that soon fades. It is not a type of self-delusion brought about by not facing reality. Nor is it the synthetic kind mirrored by fake smiles and quoted slogans. It is a calm, consistent sense of well-being because all is well with the Father.

Emmanuel assures this.

2

God with Us in *History*

Part II

Valencia, on the shore of the Mediterranean, bordered by the Turia River and secured by Roman walls, had seen many sieges but never one like this. For over a week thirty-eight Moorish kings and their formidable, combined armies had assaulted the city. Rodrigo Diaz, the commander of the forces within the city, lay sick with a fever. Though near death he knew he must plan the defense of the city and lead its forces or see his beloved land destroyed. Propped up on pillows, he worked long into the night fighting for his life and his city. At last, the strategy was complete.

As dawn's faintest rays dimly lighted the horizon the city gates opened swiftly. Before the Moors knew what was happening, Diaz, mounted on his white stallion, charged out of the city followed by his troops. With his unsheathed sword held high, he sat erect in the saddle. Swiftly 250 of the choice advance guards of the Moors were slain. His inspired followers charged on as the Diaz-mounted stallion penetrated the main camp of the enemy, causing them to rout and retreat.

Now the rising sun reflected from the sword of Diaz, and his armor glistened in its light. His preeminent presence on his white charger made him all the more imposing and inspiring to his forces as well as intimidating to the Moors. When the battle was over twenty-two of the thirty-eight Moorish kings were dead, and 10,000 of their troops killed.

It was only then the truth was known. Diaz, better known as "El Cid," completed his plan for battle and died the night before! By his order his lifeless body was braced and tied in the saddle. His presence with his troup inspired them on to victory.

His name, El Cid, came from the Arabic "El Sayyid," meaning "the lord." As a result of "the lord" being with them they were victorious. A dead man inspired their victory.

Does that illustration have to crawl on its knees and beg for understanding?

We, like the citizens of Valencia, are in an impossible position. Our leader also died. Here the parallel differs. Our Lord, though dead for three days, arose, lives, and is among us! Because He is with us, we should rejoice and claim our victory.

The virgin birth of Jesus Christ is indispensably tied to His bodily resurrection. Of Christ it was said, "a body hast thou prepared for me . . ." (Heb. 10:5). In the womb of the virgin Mary, the Father designed a body for the Son. Christ, being eternally one with the Father, could not die. Therefore, He entered an earthly form, a body, that in that body He might search for, find, and destroy death in that body. The destruction of death is called the resurrection. The citizens of the citadel of earth are safe if they will only follow "The Lord," our eternal El Cid.

Just when life gave every evidence of having only a hopeless end, Christ arose—unveiling an endless hope. Just when it appeared all was lost the angel said, "He is risen . . . He has gone before you . . ." Follow Him.

Those words were spoken at a tomb where people like us had come to bury their hope, to bid farewell to a dream, to embalm the past, and to mourn their helpless state. Even His death was part of the plan. Without it He could not conquer our strongest foe and live to lead us to victory.

For too long the world has been shouting "No" in the face of faint hope. The resurrection is God's resounding "Yes."

The world says, "No, you can't live with faith, hope, and love." In the resurrection, heaven reverberates with God's "Yes, you can!"

The world says, "No, you can't live forever." The empty tomb shouts, "Yes, you can!"

The world says, "No, you can't find a way out of the mess you are in." The Lord says, "Yes, there is a way out!"

In the scenic mountains near Colorado Springs, Colorado, an isolated road winds through Williams's Canyon to the Cave of the Winds. While hunting in the area I learned of it. The pass through which the road goes seems to become narrower and narrower as you travel up it. At one point the walls of the valley close so tightly that it is called "The Narrows." The closer you get, the more it

looks like you can't make it through. Just before you
reach that place, immediately before discouragement
prevails, there is a sign which states, "Yes you can—a
million others have."

One had to travel the pass first to show others it can
be done. Christ has shown us the way through the narrows of death. He is with us to show us the way of life.

HE TURNED PERSONS UNFIT
FOR EARTH INTO PERSONS
FIT FOR HEAVEN

The resurrected Christ said to Mary, "Go to my
brethren . . ." His brothers? Who were they?

The writer of Hebrews (2:9-11) helps us identify
them. Therein it was spoken of Him that He "tasted
death for everyone" in order to bring "many sons into
glory" and that "He is not ashamed to call them brethren." What a transformation!

Nature abounds with hints of such a transformation.

As a college student I enjoyed moments of escape on
a lazy Louisiana bayou. I would pole a pirogue into a
remote area and while away the afternoon studying for a
test and researching nature. The waters of the bayou
were colored dark from the tannic acid caused by decaying vegetation.

One day as I looked over the side of the boat, I no-
ticed a number of large water bugs crawling around in
the slime of the decaying matter on the bottom. Slowly,
one crawled out of the water onto the end of the boat. I
remained motionless at first and watched. Soon we were

acclimated to each other, and motion seemed not to bother him. I continued to study but took intermittent glances at him. The sun slowly dried his outer shell. Almost imperceptibly, a hairline crack developed down his back. As it gradually widened a new creature emerged from the dry, dead outer shell. The new lovely creature sat for a while on the old shell. Gingerly it lifted its frail wings and stretched them. This he did again and again. Finally he fluttered them several times. Eventually he flapped his gossamer wings, and the new creature was propelled into space.

The rays of the sun were caught by his wings and reflected all the beautiful colors of the rainbow. Then I looked back in the water, and there were its old companions still in the mire. The only difference in them and him was he had been born again. He was now equipped for the heavens. No longer was he suited for the low life.

Because of The Emmanuel Factor we too can experience new life. Once unfit for earth we can be suited for heaven.

As radical as that thought sounds, it is a Bible-based fact. By our repentant faith Christ becomes our brother. As a result of salvation you are as good as Christ. No, not really, but yes, actually. You are as righteous as Christ. Remember, He is the perfectly righteous Son of God. When a believer receives Him, then His righteousness is imputed, that is, credited to the believer's account. Christ's righteousness becomes that of the believer.

Thus, in the eyes of God the Father we become the righteousness of God in Christ. Positionally, that is "in

Christ," you are in the eyes of the Father as good as Christ. Experientially you certainly are not. We can do nothing of ourselves to earn, merit, or deserve this classification. It is a gift imputed to our account. The Father could not and would not take anyone into His holy presence who is not holy. Because of The Emmanuel Factor you enter into His presence by virtue of the fact you are in Christ, and His righteousness is credited to your account. In union with Christ, positionally the Father sees you as holy as Christ.

That positional truth should impact our experiential conduct. Being unchained from the chariot wheels of the world we should seek to show forth His grace by our lifestyle. It does not impress the world if we profess our positional perfection and then show the disposition of a top sergeant whose shoes are too tight.

We who dine at God's smorgasbord of blessings must be transparent and authentic if we expect to attract a disbelieving world to Christ.

The fact of Christ's bodily resurrection transformed lives in the era of the epoch, and it still does today. His grand coming-out party on history's horizon influences all others. Every argument against His resurrection is philosophical. Every argument for it is historical.

The famous Greek scholar, Bishop Westcott, wrote:

> Taking all the evidence together, it is not too much to say that there is no other single historic incident better or more variously supported than the resurrection of Christ.

Medical Doctor Luke, who wrote when people who were in Jerusalem at the time of the resurrection were still living, after writing of it, concluded, "You are witnesses of these things" (Luke 24:48).

Luke further wrote of the resurrection, "There are many infallible proofs." This translates *tekmerion* meaning "demonstrable proofs," that is, much emperical evidence.

Writing in that same timespan the author of Acts (2:32) noted, "This Jesus God has raised up, of which we are all witnesses."

This historical happening made an impact on believers that thrust them into heavenly orbit.

James, the half-brother of our Lord, was a skeptic before the resurrection. He is listed as a witness of the fact. It so changed his life and emboldened him that he became head of the emerging church and died because of His belief in the supernatural bodily resurrection of Christ. He was made fit for heaven and enabled to serve in time.

In the first century, a time when they should have known, belief in the resurrection was so broadspread and firmly believed that over 5,000,000 were executed because of their faith. Though belittled and beleaguered by the world they maintained a constant faith. The author of Hebrews (11:35-38) made this observation of this heaven-bound band:

> And others were tortured, not accepting deliverance, that they might obtain a better

resurrection. Still others had trial of mockings and scourgings, yes, and of chains and imprisonments. They were stoned, they were sawn in two, were tempted, were slain with the sword. They wandered about in sheepskins and goatskins, being destitute, afflicted, tormented—of whom the world was not worthy.

Heaven awaited those of which "the world was not worthy."

His resurrection has added two new equations to the only one known until that time. The three equations are:

$$L + D + D = D$$

Life, physical life;
> plus spiritual death;
> plus physical death; equals
> > eternal death (that is, separation
> > from God and His love for eternity).

Physical life without the hope of eternal life makes for a hopeless life. German Count Otto von Bismarck once said, "Without the hope of eternal life, this life is not worth the effort of getting dressed in the morning."

$$L + L + D = L$$

Life, physical life;
> plus life, spiritual life;
> plus death, physical death; equals
> > eternal life.

" . . . we shall be saved by His life" (Rom. 5:10). "His life" is a reference to His resurrected life. Because He lives we shall live forever.

Time magazine stated, "We have a great fear of dying and yet we are unable to face the reality of death."

Facing the fact of death encourages one to choose the correct equation for life. This we must do because, "It is appointed unto man once to die" (Heb. 9:27). With Christ as Savior, we can face death because He promised, "Because I live you shall live also" (John 14:19).

Because of the literal, historical bodily resurrection of Christ there is a third potential equation.

$$L + L + L = L$$

Life, physical life;
plus life, spiritual life;
plus life, raptured or resurrected life;
equals life eternal.

The resurrection of Christ validates His claim that He will come again. Therefore, there is the appropriate appeal to ". . . wait for His Son from heaven, whom He raised from the dead, that is Jesus, who delivers us from the wrath to come" (1 Thess. 1:10).

Because He arose, those of us who die before His next coming shall also be resurrected at His coming. "He who raised Christ from the dead will also give life to your mortal bodies" (Rom. 8:11).

The last two equations are only for those who have

allowed Him to prepare them for heaven. The fact He is Emmanuel, God with us, means we someday will be with Him in His Father's house of many mansions.

HE TURNED A PEOPLE
UNABLE TO COPE
INTO A PEOPLE OF HOPE

Despair gripped His disillusioned followers. In dread hopelessness they hid in fear. One of the best proofs of the resurrection is found in the change made in these cowardly lives when they who doubted were convinced He was alive. They who doubted there was a future for them could not face one if there were one. Many find themselves in that same position today.

As the fifteenth century was nearing an end all of Europe was caught in the chilly labyrinth of hopelessness. The mood captured the mood of many in every generation. Despair and defeat had led to dismay. So depressed were the masses that a common belief was held that a hopeless end of the world was coming soon.

The Nuremburg Chronicle was authored by Hartmann Schedel, a German writer, in 1493. In his work the author cataloged the calamities that had beset humanity to that date. At the end of the book he fatalistically left a blank page and invited his readers to record additional disasters that would happen before the soon-coming end of the world.

The next year a sailing ship with a bold young man at its helm sailed into Lisbon harbor. The crew of that battered little vessel brought news of an adventure too fascinating to be true. They had braved the tempest of the vast unchartered Atlantic to bring news of a new land. Theirs was the story of a new world, pregnant with possibility, abounding in potential, and full of hope.

The lightbearer, Christopher Columbus, spoke not of despair in tones of hopelessness. His was not talk about the end of the world but about an endless hope.

The maps by which he sailed showed an ominous caption just off the British and European coasts: *Ne Plus Ultra*, meaning "No more beyond." Further out on the edge of the vast unknown were such perilous inscriptions as "Here be dragons." These hope-defeating giants were overcome and the maps changed to read *Plus Ultra*, meaning "Much more beyond."

Christ's emergence from the grave gives hope because we now know there is much more beyond even the grave. This plus is part of the superabundant additive He gives life here and now.

Peter and John went to Christ's tomb, typifying the mood of their generation which was not dissimilar to that of our day. They came away full of endless hope. A new world had been discovered. There was life beyond the grave and now abundant life in time.

Our word "hope" came from a combination of two old Anglo-Saxon word meanings: desire plus expectation. When a person feels hopeless, desire and a sense of expectancy are lost. Conversely, clinical studies have shown that when someone knows a person or persons have a desire for them to achieve and fully expect them to, they are motivated and more likely to achieve. Motivation is lacking in the lives of those who have no one who believes in them enough to desire their good and to expect the best from them.

We should be motivated by knowing Christ desires our good and expects from us our best. That fans hope into open flame.

The noted American cardiologist, Dr. R. McNair Wilson, in his biography, *Doctor's Progress*, stated, "Hope is the medicine I use more than any other . . . Hope can cure nearly anything."

Hope, he says, is medicinal. The influence of hope on our emotions, physical well-being, psychological disposition, and spiritual life is well documented. Christ gives that hope.

Dr. Harold G. Wolff, professor of medicine at Cornell University Medical College, did extensive research into the impact upon American soldiers held in Nazi prison camps during World War II. He wrote:

> In short, prolonged circumstances which are perceived as dangerous, as lonely, as hopeless, may drain a man of hope and of his health; but he is capable of enduring incredible burdens and taking cruel punishment when he has self-esteem, hope, purpose, and belief in his fellows.

Much in our culture holds some persons captive as a mad Hitler did his victims. Christ has come to set the prisoner free. When the door of His tomb was opened, the gateway to hope also swung wide. His followers of

the first century flooded through it to turn the world up-
side down. He enables us, as He did them, to face reality
and overcome circumstances through hope.

Some people are like the young woman who happened upon a terrible accident. The scene was horrible;
bodies were broken and blood was all over the place. She
commented, "I have never been more thankful for my
first aid training. When I saw the conditions of those
people I remembered my training. Immediately I sat
down and put my head between my knees so I wouldn't
faint."

The ostrich formula for facing life's problems
doesn't work. Christ alone can help us face them.

There are those today who are just hanging on, trying to avoid fainting because of the mess of life that sur-
rounds them. Jesus can change that. The circumstances
are not necessarily what He will change, but He can and
will change the individual to cope with the situation.

Our hope is *Christocentric*. In writing to young
Timothy, his mentor Paul distilled this thought into four
words, "Jesus Christ our hope" (1 Tim. 1:1).

When we have a strong desire to please Him and an
expectant will that we can, we are motivated. When we
know He has strong desire to aid us and unlimited resources He expects us to use, we are catalysed.

Our hope is not in some pollyanna program or panacea prescription; it is in the person Jesus Christ; not in
what we can do but in Who He is—Emmanuel, God
with us.

Those familiar with the condition of the average college dorm room can appreciate this analogy. Some college students had stolen the mascot of a neighboring school—a goat. They had made elaborate plans for sneaking it into their room. Someone asked, "What about the smell?" Candidly came this reply, "The goat will just have to get used to it."

Jesus does not come into our life to "get used to it." He comes to get us used to a new life-style full of hope.

Hope as afforded by Christ is genuine, valid, and productive. It is not false hope as spoken of by Job (27:8), "For what is the hope of the hypocrite . . . when God takes away his life?" Hype, self-dynamics, egotism, blind enthusiasm, and energy of the flesh afford superficial and hypocritical hope. When it comes down to the basic nitty and fundamental gritty, there is no hope apart from Christ. Apart from Christ, people are "without hope and without God in this world" (Eph. 2:12).

This condition results in a hopeless state. The Psalmist (43:5) mused over this: "Why are you cast down, O my soul? And why are you disquieted within me? Hope in God . . ."

Christians encounter discouragement. Extenuating circumstances, conflicts, and various pressures are a part of life. Older members of the German society have an expression used when they are at the end of the rope. They say, "We have come to the last chapter of Matthew." Some think this means they have come to the end of everything, when despair takes over. However, their reference is to the great truth contained therein that renews them. Matthew concludes with Jesus saying, "Lo, I am with you always, even to the end of the age" (Matt. 28:20). Rejoice, Emmanuel is here! He is the God of hope!

"Now the God of hope fill you with joy and peace in believing, that you may abound in hope . . ." (Rom. 15:13).

Two triumphant truths stimulate our hope.

One is His word. "For whatever things were written . . . that we through the patience and comfort of the Scripture might have hope" (Rom. 15:4).

The second is a primary truth found in His Word. It is the marvel of the resurrection. He "has begotten us again unto a living hope of the resurrection of Jesus Christ" (1 Pet. 1:3).

Perspective often determines the degree of our hope. A fertile imagination would allow us to hear onlookers' comments as David went out to face Goliath, "Look how much bigger Goliath is than David." Meanwhile, David chortled as he thought, "Look how much smaller Goliath is than my God."

When you next size up a challenge or a problem, measure it by the size of God.

HE TURNED A PLACE OF DEATH INTO A PLACE OF LIFE

The horror of death still haunts the unenlightened mind. Those without Christ find the idea of the grave reason for despair. Readily it can be conceded that superficially it is one of the most likely settings for anguish and agony. Apart from Christ, human death represents humanity's greatest defeat and ultimate loss.

Christ's resurrection changed this. For a person who has received Christ as Savior, it is "The End." The front end—of glory. By the resurrection dawning's early light the grave became a symbol of heaven's triumph. It means He is still with us—Emmanuel.

Death's night sky would be starless and its day hopeless were it not for Christ's exaltation, "I am He who lives, and was dead, and behold, I am alive forevermore" (Rev. 1:18).

Victor Hugo voiced the hope with which many approach the grave. "When I go down to the grave I can say, like so many others: I have finished my work, but I cannot say I have finished my life. My day's work will begin the next morning. My tomb is not a blind alley. It is a thoroughfare. It closes in the twilight to open in the dawn."

Christ made the old door of death into a revolving door. His brief bodily trip back was to assure us that He "will never leave us." Spiritual strength within the believer is proportionate to the extent the person is able to absorb the fact of His presence. Those who acknowledge His presence and accept the fact of His invisible presence sense His presence. This awareness is an enablement leading to victory.

The thrill is: He is with us. The tragedy is many never really avail themselves of the hope associated with His beloved presence. Those who don't fall apart, panic, grow weary, and become negative. Their favorite verse might well be:

> When in trouble,
> When in doubt;
> Run in circles,
> Scream and shout.

The Light of the world now shines to guild the mountaintops of your achievements and light the valleys of your defeats. Because He lives He makes the habitat of physical and spiritual death a place of life.

Dachau was a name of mystery. This World War II German death camp was a place of despicable horror and tragic death. Here Nazi terror reigned from 1933 until 1945. Hundreds of thousands of persons were subjected to unbearable working conditions, torture, punishment, starvation, and execution. Grassy forbidden areas bordered the inside of the high fences topped with electric barbed wire. It was a place of death. Massive ovens were used to cremate bodies. All who entered there abandoned hope.

When World War II ended, the prison was vacated and left empty. Those captives under the penalty of death were liberated.

At the same time hundreds of refugees fleeing from Communism in east Europe had no place to go. The abandoned camp at Dachau was cleaned up and opened as temporary housing for many of these. The place of horror and death became a place of life and a new beginning. That which had meant despair now offered *hope*.

In His resurrection Jesus did the same for the grave. It now is a place of hope also. However, the analogy can be pressed further. Those held in bondage by the world are also set free even while in the world.

Appropriately Paul wrote: "Death is swallowed up in victory. O Death, Where is thy sting? O Grave, where is thy victory . . . Thanks be to God, which giveth us the victory through our Lord . . ." Our Lord—Emmanuel!

3

God with Us in *Hedonism*

Nestled in a valley of the upper Rhine River, between Austria and Switzerland, is the world's fourth smallest country, Liechtenstein. This tiny sixty-two-square-mile principality has been ruled over by the Hapsburg family for about 265 years. In 1984, Crown Prince Franz Joseph II relinquished his throne to his son, thus ending Europe's longest modern reign. The popularity of Franz Joseph II is in part attributable to the fact he was their first ruler who actually lived permanently in Liechtenstein. All of his predecessors had ruled from the comfort of distant Vienna. His success resulted from his electing to live among his people in his country's capital of Vaduz.

Well might we sing of Emmanuel:

> Thou didst leave Thy throne and Thy kingly crown, when Thou camest to earth for me.

Thus, The Emmanuel Factor is at work in our hedonistic society.

Many avow and others aspire to a philosophy called hedonism. The word itself may not be known but the philosophy is. Hedonism comes from the Greek word meaning "pleasure." In ancient Greece, the Cyrenaics based their ethical philosophies on the idea that pleasure is the highest good. Good is defined in light of the pleasure it affords. Our secular society is schooled in this ideology. Entertainment, education, advertising, and ethics are pleasure-centered.

Product quality in advertising is incidental. What pleasure does it give? Gas mileage, performance, horsepower, and torque are incidental. If it is a "fun truck" it sells. Sensuality is superior in importance to cost, quality, or durability.

Fulfillment is advocated to be found in things. Get a sportier car, take an exotic trip, buy a new wardrobe, or move into a fancier dwelling, and happiness will be yours. That is the constant media hype. Bland faces, empty lives, meaningless existence, guilt complexes, and broken relationships are silent confessions that all this is a lie.

Self-pampering consumerism has taken the place of self-discipline. Our survivalist mentality espouses self-fulfillment, not self-denial. Self-absorption, not self-giving, is a symptom of our narcissism.

If we do not use our *hindsight* we will be deficient in *insight*, and that reduces *foresight*. Hedonism's "me" and "now" syndrome bleaches initiative out of lives, erodes objectivity, robs one of moral integrity, and strips persons of concern for others and society in general. In all forms it always has and always will.

Lord Devlin, the famous British jurist, observed: "A sense of right and wrong is necessary for the life of a community . . . History shows that the loosening of moral bonds is often the first stage of society's disintegration."

Jesus Christ dealt with both the root and fruit of sin. We have a tendency to deal with the fruit punitively. That is, we punish offenders after the fact. Jesus desires to deal preventively with the root of sin. Though He forgives guilt He prefers to prevent grief. In this vein He warned against "looking and lusting."

The pattern was established in the Garden of Eden. Eve "saw the tree was good for food, that it was pleasant to the eyes . . ." Sin number one came as a result of a glance in the wrong direction which incited a craving for personal pleasure to the expense of all else.

Israel was defeated by a numerically inferior force because one of Joshua's soldiers "saw" a gold wedge and stole it in violation of God's command.

David, a man after God's own heart, "saw Bathsheba" and sin ensued.

The human eye is the gateway to the will. We have a tendency to enact what entices us. Vision is often the first of the five senses incited causing allurement. It has the greatest perimeter of all the senses and the most immediate admission into the mind.

THE CONDITION

Two areas of study which reveal our hedonistic preoccupation are pornography and fornication. One is fantasy-oriented and the other reality-related.

Pornography

Newsstands are pregnant with publications that exploit nudity for purely erotic purposes. Pornography in America is an $8 billion business annually. There are approximately 20,000 adult book stores in the U.S. with average monthly gross receipts of between $10,000 and $20,000 each.

According to a U.S. government study, nearly three-quarters of all such material is prepared for children under 18. It is estimated that more than 70 percent of all such material ends up in a minor's possession. Each year over 800 soft-core and hard-core issues alone sell a total of over 200 million copies. Two hundred and seventy-five monthly publications deal with child porn.

The "eye gate" is further flooded in 800 adult movie houses attended by two and one-half million viewers. Over 500,000 different porno video cassettes have been sold. Television producers are showing Americans 20,000 scenes (2.7 per hour) of sex outside of marriage annually. Eighty-eight percent of all sex on television is outside of marriage.

In the name of "broadmindedness" some argue that it is a matter of degree in defending certain magazines. *Playboy*, *Penthouse*, and *Hustler* are three often offered this defense.

A look at these three glitzy publications from the standpoint of pedophilia alone is revealing. Pedophilia is a form of child abuse. It involves adults and children engaged sexually. Such extreme conduct is still looked upon by most of society as abhorrent.

Judith Reisman, a researcher at American University, did an exhaustive study in which her staff analyzed the photographic or cartoon sexual involvement of children in these publications. They found 6,004 images linking children with sex.

Hustler had an average of 14.1 per issue; *Playboy*—8.2, and *Penthouse*—6.4.

Fantasies have a tendency to become facts. Attitudes become actions. What you see is what you get—to be.

Fornication

The world condones immorality and glamorizes promiscuity, but God says He will judge it: "fornicators and adulterers God will judge" (Heb. 13:4).

"Adulterers" translates the Greek word *moichos* and means unlawful intercourse with the spouse of another.

"Fornication" translates *pornos* and means illicit sexual intercourse. It included adultery but much more. It encompasses pre- and extra-marital relations between married and unmarried men with women, women with women, and men with men.

Today whatever is popular is permissible. This mandate for mediocrity is taking us into a desert of depravity.

Many are marrying at much earlier ages. Two of five brides are teenagers. Of these one of every two is pregnant. If the groom is a teenager, there is an 80 percent chance his bride is pregnant.

Approximately 20 percent of our 15-year-olds have had sex. Of the teens who become pregnant, 45 percent elect to abort. Of those who become pregnant, 30 percent are pregnant again within a year.

The divorce rate among teens who marry is three times higher than among other age groups.

Abortion

These individuals "receive in themselves the penalty of their error which was due" (Rom. 1:27). Two ways in which God judges people in their own bodies as a result of promiscuity is with unwanted pregnancies and disease.

The most dangerous place in America today is a mother's womb. Sexual promiscuity causes many untimely and undesired pregnancies. Becoming promiscuous is a primary pleasure sought in our nation. Yet being pregnant causes much unhappiness. Being a pleasure-seeking society, the by-product of pleasure, pregnancy, is often cast away. The word "abort(ion)" defined in *Webster's Encyclopedia of Dictionaries* means "to fail to bring to fruition." When a preborn baby is aborted, it is the human life principle that is not allowed to come to fruition.

That which is aborted is a human being. It surely must be conceded that it is a being. It is there so it surely is not a non-being. Since it results from copulation by two human beings, it is human. It is undeniably there. It is obviously human. It is not a nonentity or a non-human species; it is rather a preborn human being.

Every day in America 4,300 preborn babies are aborted. That is an annual total of 1.5 million. Slightly more than one percent of these are performed because of life-threatening reasons. In order to get back in the pleasure chase they are performed for convenience.

This is a blood battle being waged. It is the most costly war ever fought in America, according to human life loss. Consider the casualties:

Revolutionary War	25,324
Civil War	498,332
World War I	116,710
World War II	407,316
Korean War	54,546
Vietnam War	58,098
War of the Unborn	9,500,000+

When French sculptor Bartholdi was planning and working for nearly twenty years on the Statue of Liberty, he chose as his model his own mother. Motherhood needs a revitalized image in our day.

Who are these people not being allowed to come to fruition?

C. S. Lewis noted: "It is immortals whom we joke with, work with, marry, snub, and exploit. Immortal horrors or everlasting splendors." The key word is "immortals."

Some critical skeptics refer to the preborn as "fetal matter" which they do not consider a human being until it starts breathing. Let's take that narrow definition as a guideline.

"Luke the beloved physician" (Col. 4:14), writing under divine inspiration, called such unborn infants *brephos*. This is a Greek term meaning "a breathing infant." Doctor Luke also used the same term to describe Christ after birth. Naturally the question arises, "How could a preborn be considered 'a breathing thing'?"

Modern science has finally answered that question. The answer is that the fetus both "breathes" and receives nourishment through the umbilical cord coming from the placenta. An example of this is found in open-heart surgery known as "cardiopulmonary bypass." Although the lungs of the persons undergoing the operation are artificially ventilated during the procedure to prevent them from collapsing, they do not oxygenate the blood during the surgery. This has to be done mechanically because the patient "breathes through the blood." In like manner the preborn breathes through the blood of the mother.

These people not being allowed to come to fruition are living, breathing human beings.

David wrote: "I am fearfully and wonderfully made; Marvelous are Your works" (Ps. 139:14).

This statement was penned long before David had cause to know his body consisted of 30 trillion cells, each with twenty-three chromosomes all of which have a memory. At the moment of conception the genes are present that determine whether you will be an ecto-morph, tall person; endomorph, fat person; or a meso-morph, in between. Innate in those genes at the instant of conception are the color of your hair, eyes, and skin, and your sex. Eighteen weeks later all organs are formed, as are the fingers and toes. A human being is in the process of emerging.

Who are these people being aborted?

A well-known case follows. Ask yourself as you consider this case if you would have recommended an abortion.

The mother was pregnant with her fifth child. Her husband had syphilis, and she tuberculosis. Their first child was born blind. Their second child died shortly after birth. Their third child was deaf. Their fourth child had tuberculosis. Would you have advised aborting the fifth child?

If so, you just suggested aborting Ludwig van Beethoven.

Rape is often used as an appeal for abortion. Such a potential mother should live with the awareness that the child is not the responsible party. Have you ever thrilled to the music of Ethel Waters? Fortunately her mother, who was a rape victim, did not opt for abortion.

When a woman considers an abortion, she should ask the same question posed by the prophet Micah (6:7), "Shall I give my first-born for my transgressions, the fruit of my body for the sin of my soul?"

Of one the Lord said, "Now the word of the Lord came to me saying, Before I formed you in the womb, I knew you, and before you were born, I consecrated you; I have appointed you a prophet to the nations" (Jer. 1:4-5). If that baby had been aborted, it would have been the prophet Jeremiah who later said, "My mother might have been my grave" if he had died in the womb (Jer. 20:17).

Homosexuality

Another symptom of our sin sickness is male homosexuality and female homosexuality (lesbianism). Even if sex between consenting partners of the same sex were considered proper, it would still be fornication because it is not a relationship between husband and wife. In some states it is a felony as defined by the U.S. Supreme Court.

Today there are a number of terms used to describe sodomites. Some are gay, fairy, fag, queer, or homosexual. The Bible uses fifteen different terms to refer to such an act.

Sodomy (Gen. 19:4-10; 1 Kings 14:24;
    2 Kings 23:7).
Abomination (Lev. 18:22; Deut. 22:5).
Vile affections (Rom. 1:26,27).
Burning with lust (Rom. 1:27).
Dishonoring the body (Rom. 1:24).
Violating nature (Rom. 1:26).
Shameful lusts (Rom. 1:27).
Wickedness (Judges 19:23).
Lusting for strange flesh (Jude 1:7).
Filthy dreamers (Jude 1:8).
Abusers of themselves (1 Cor. 6:9).
Effeminate (1 Cor. 6:9).
Defilers of themselves (1 Tim. 1:9-10).

Inordinate (Col. 3:5-6).
Reprobate (Rom. 1:28).

Our word homosexuality is not a Bible term. It is man's term intended to remove the moral and spiritual connotations of sin. The act is unconditionally condemned by those terms.

In light of God's Word speaking of them "receiving in themselves the penalty of their error which was due," the question arises regarding AIDS being such discipline.

The answer: "Yes and no."

Yes, it is a natural consequence of an act God in His Word has condemned.

No, it is not a direct discipline for all homosexuality.

If it were a direct punishment, all homosexuals and only homosexuals would have it. Other victims of AIDS are drug-takers who use dirty needles, prostitutes, hemophiliacs who require blood transfusions, and children born to infected parents. There are innocent victims in that list. If AIDS were only a punishment for sodomy those would not have it.

Regarding the "yes" answer it is hard to overlook Romans 1:18, "For the wrath of God is revealed from heaven against all ungodliness and unrighteousness of men, who suppress the truth in unrighteousness."

"Let no one deceive you with empty words, for because of such things God's wrath comes on those who are disobedient" (Eph. 5:6).

One "who sins sexually sins against his own body" (1 Cor. 6:18).

THE CAUSE

Having examined the fruit now consider the root.

Wisdom of the ages is contained in Proverbs 27:20 which states: "Hell and destruction are never full; so the eyes of man are never satisfied."

The eye may be the portal by which immoral activities are stimulated. Some advocate saturating the market with publically condoned pornography so society will become desensitized and abuse will be diminished. In the proverb stated, Solomon wisely opposed such action. That is like trying to eat enough on Thanksgiving to last for the full year. It won't last, but by enlarging the stomach, by overindulgence, a greater appetite results. The same is true of sensual stimuli.

Law enforcement officials can backtrack sex-murder criminals. The digression that leads to such crimes has as its point of entry pornography. The *Chicago Sun-Times* carried a report which revealed that 77 percent of those who molest boys and 87 percent of those who molest girls admitted emulating the sexual behavior they had seen in erotic materials.

The respected *New England Journal of Medicine* claims clinical proof linking observation and response. They have documented a significant upswing in teen suicides following news reports or movies on the subject. Copycat suicides were up 40 percent above normal in New York City among teens during a two-week period following broadcasting of four made-for-TV movies on the subject.

Why?

"The eye is not satisfied with seeing . . ." (Eccl. 1:8) is the simple answer. Like Solomon, Seneca helps explain the cause: "No man is free if he is slave to the flesh."

Our current low view of human life as revealed by our willingness to abort children has its root in one of the earliest proponents of Hedonism. Aristippus, a philosopher who lived around 400 BC, was an early proponent of the pleasure pursuit at all cost. A friend encouraged him to show his own children more affection as a result of them having come "from his own loins." He responded by spitting and commenting that excrement also came from him, and that we also engender worms and lice. He was more concerned about his own pleasure than about his role as a parent.

Such a base expression is repulsive. Even more abhorrent is our conduct in disposing of the fruit of the womb as though it is mere excrement.

THE CONSEQUENCE

Having sown to the wind too long we are just beginning to reap the whirlwind. A recent FBI report estimates that one out of four 12-year-old girls will be raped in her lifetime unless something is immediately done about pornography.

Dr. Armand Nicoli, a psychiatrist for Harvard University, spoke to the reality of libertine pleasures: "This is what a psychiatrist sees—unwanted pregnancies, ill-advised marriages, abortions followed by severe depressions and haunting repetitive nightmares, disillusionment, frustration, despondency, suicide. It is for this reason that psychiatrists are concerned about what is happening. It is for this reason that many of them are convinced that something is wrong somewhere. This new sexual freedom is not what people are led to believe."

One of the nation's most respected researchers, Psychologist Edward Donnerstein of the University of Wisconsin, conducted an extensive study of the influence of pornographic violence on the attitude of men toward women. As a result, he concluded that a heavy diet of sexually violent movies (even R-rated ones) desensitizes men toward violence and makes them consider rape trivial.

Dolf Zillman of the University of Indiana, another premier researcher, studied the effects on viewers of nonviolent pornographic movies. His study found that men begin to consider women insatiable sexual playthings. These men are more aggressive toward women and begin to consider rape as a trivial offense secretly desired by most women.

Zillman concluded, "There can be no doubt that pornography, as a form of primarily male entertainment, promotes victimization of women."

Our Hedonistic culture gives youth an unrealistic, if not perverted, concept of sex. Its negative impact causes later married life to be distorted. It presents an unreal view of human sexuality. If a husband or wife sees this exaggerated and fantasized perspective as the norm the reality of marriage will be damaged.

The consequence of AIDS being spread more rapidly by the sodomistic section of society than any other is potentially devastating. Over one million persons are estimated now to be infected with the AIDS virus. Within five years it is estimated that there will be over 2,700,000 cases. The rate of increase from there is frightening.

We have sown within our society our own seeds of potential destruction. Prevention of further sowing is always decried when proposed. "Censorship" or "legalism" is shouted. Liberty is the mandate.

We have rules, regulations, limitations, and laws in many areas of our community life. Why not in these domains? We have laws governing our rate of speed, limitations of the air waves, guidelines for employment, taxation on our income, and controls on what we can mail.

Dr. Francis J. Braceland, former president of the American Psychiatric Association, said, "Premarital sex relations resulting from the so-called new morality have greatly increased the number of young people in mental hospitals."

Dr. Eric Fromm, the internationally noted psychoanalyst, said the current sexual freedoms in no way contribute to a true sense of aliveness or richness or experience. There is a frustrating emptiness which follows.

The late Clarence Edward McCartney spoke summarily of the result of Hedonism's fruit: "The laws of God are given for man's good and perfection, and wherever violated they bring suffering. Prophylactics may save from physical disease; and contraceptives from children; but there is no prophylactic which can save the mind from contamination or the soul from tarnish, and there is no contraceptive which will prevent the conception of children of regret, self-despising, and self-degradation."

THE CORRECTIVE

Arnold Toynbee based his conclusion on an analytical study of nineteen formerly great nations. He observed: "No nation has ever survived that failed to discipline itself sexually."

Edith Hamilton, respected Greek historian, made this comment on the land that gave us Hedonism: "When the freedom they wished for most was the freedom from responsibility, then Athens ceased to be free and was never free again."

Jesus Christ said, ". . . if your right eye causes you to sin, pluck it out and cast it from you." We get so absorbed in defending the right eye from literally being plucked out that we forget the emphasis Christ was putting on getting rid of the source of temptation. Of course, He doesn't want the eye extracted from our head. However, in using that graphic phrase He was dramatizing how expedient it is to remove a source of temptation. Only as we do so personally and individually will we have a basis for a society willing to do so.

Studies in sensory perception reveal that 82 percent of what you remember comes through the eye and 14 percent through the ear. The first step toward correcting the problem is to remove the root. Conclude with the Psalmist, "I will set nothing wicked before my eyes" (101:3).

We have become "lovers of pleasure rather than lovers of God" (2 Tim. 3:4), and are bent on ". . . serving various lusts and pleasures" (Titus 3:3). Pretense that there is no pleasure in sin must be abandoned. The Word of God speaks of persons who "enjoy the passing pleasures of sin" (Heb. 11:25). Certain sins are exhilarating. Fleshly appetites and sensuous drives can give momentary thrills.

The source of our choice of pleasures determines their desirability and durability. David, who had to eat the bitter fruit as a result of choosing the wrong source, later returned to experience the true pleasure which comes from pleasing the Lord. He wrote: "At Your right hand are pleasures forevermore" (Ps. 16:11).

For The Emmanuel Factor to be a factor, our pleasure-seeking, "I"-centered kingdom must undergo a revolution. Only when Christ is enthroned can one live morally pure in our sensate society. Passion must be restrained and trained while propriety and purity must be unashamedly unshackled. "I"-ness must no longer be left alone to guard our impulses and emotions.

The Emmanuel Factor will give victory. The fruit of the Spirit is "love, joy, peace . . . self-control . . ." (Gal. 5:22-23). Only when our individual will is under the control of Christ can there be self-control.

Our pursuit of pleasure is a search for a person or thing to give what God alone can give. His pleasures are "forevermore." Those who seek to please Him are awakened to find the beautiful by-product, their own joy, peace, happiness, and . . . pleasure.

When The Emmanuel Factor is at work we will gladly "flee youthful lusts" (1 Cor. 6:18). The word "flee" means to run so fast we kick up dust. A strategic retreat often leads to victory. George Washington was a poor general according to some military strategists. This conclusion is reached because of his many retreats. He didn't mind giving up ground in order to win the war. He was a genius! Our objective should be to win every battle in our spiritual warfare. Retreat is often necessary for there to be an advance.

King David camped in the heat of the sun at Adullam. His battle had been long and hard fought. In a quiet moment his reveries caused him to think of his hometown of Bethlehem. Thirst caused him to draw from his well of memories the fresh cool water of Bethlehem's water well.

Some of his men later heard him speaking of how he craved a drink from that well. At the peril of their lives they slipped through enemy lines and went back to Bethlehem to get some of this much-desired water. David wanted it more than they wanted their own lives. When David was made a gift of this pleasure-giving drink he did so with delight. Then respectfully he poured it out on the desert sand as a sacrifice to God. In that same spirit Paul wrote: "I beseech you therefore, brethren, by the mercies of God, that you present your bodies a living sacrifice, holy, acceptable to God, which is your reasonable service. And do not be conformed to this world, but be transformed by the renewing of your mind, that you may prove what is that good and acceptable and perfect will of God" (Rom. 12:1-2).

The Emmanuel Factor worked in Corinth. The church there consisted of converted fornicators, idolaters, adulterers, homosexuals, sodomists, thieves, covetous men, blasphemers, drunkards, and extortioners (1 Cor. 6:9-10). It can work in America. To think of changing America one life at a time may be a great act of faith. To try to do it any other way is a greater act of futility.

4

God with Us in *Harmony*

A reporter for the New York Times sat on a ridge overlooking the Civil War battle at Cedar Creek. As the Union forces were being routed he wrote: "I am witnessing the terrible dissolution of the Union."

General Philip H. "Little Phil" Sheridan, their commanding officer, was at Winchester when fighting erupted. At full gallop he rode the eleven miles back to the battlefield. With his banner unfurled he rode into the battle at full speed, shouting to his men: "Sheridan is here. Here is Sheridan. Follow me, and we will win the victory."

They did—and they did.

The elevation of inspiration derived from an individual or ideal is inestimable.

Jesus Christ rode into earth's spiritual warfare on the winds of heaven with the angels saying: "Emmanuel is here. God is with us. Follow Him and win the victory." Those who have—have.

Sheridan's presence rallied his divided forces. His very being gave them incentive to respond as one unit.

Together they were a formidable force. As a harmonious unit they prevailed. Victory was theirs.

This togetherness was spoken of by Paul who, in referring to Christ and His followers, noted we "may grow up in all things into Him who is the head—Christ—from whom the whole body, joined and knit together by what every joint supplies, according to the effective working by which every part does its share, causes growth of the body for the edifying of itself in love" (Eph. 4:15,16).

This summary text suggests four things achieved by being together in Christ. This is true in a family or church.

> UNIFYING—"joined together"
> SUPPLYING—"every joint supplies"
> EDIFYING—"effective working . . . edifying"
> MULTIPLYING—"causes growth"

This expression from the Greek theater had application in the emerging church as well as the body today. In drama the Greeks excelled. One stage prop used was a primitive form of a crane. If an actor was to depict the mighty Zeus, a small rope was attached to a harness under the actor's robe. This in turn was tied to the crane. By turning wheels and cogs the crane would move the suspended Zeus over the stage as though he were flying.

Occasionally these primitive machines would break down. If the cogs did not mesh just right, catastrophe consequented. Having gotten the flying Zeus on stage in a suspended fashion there was no way to get him off. Greek audiences had a classy way of getting rid of overripe fruit and vegetables. In the moments that followed the mighty Zeus would get plastered with rotten produce.

Applied to the Christian community this is an appeal not to let a person who is fulfilling his role get hung up, exposed, and abused because of the body not being cognate, that is, working together. We are to assist and to aid one another. When the body works in harmony, support results.

HEAVEN'S HARMONY

Harmony in music well illustrates what it means for persons to live together in harmony. Harmony in music is the study of musical chords and their relationships. A chord consists of two or more tones sounded at the same time. These are even regular vibrations. Irregular vibrations of clashing pitches are called cacophony, meaning chaotic sound, or noise.

To develop harmony a basic pitch must be established. It happens when notes get together at the same time. Determining the basic pitch, same key, is fundamental to harmony.

In personal or intragroup relationships Jesus is the universal "basic pitch." Fundamental doctrines are the equivalent of even, regular vibrations. Jesus, The Emmanuel Factor, is essential for harmony socially, intellectually, morally, and spiritually. When a group makes "doctrinal sounds together" there is harmony.

Charlie Pritchett is one of the South's foremost piano tuners. He says it is virtually impossible to tune two pianos with each other. However, by using a tuning fork one can be tuned. By using the same tuning fork the other can then be tuned with it. The result is that the two pianos are tuned together. The tuning fork assures the basic pitch to be the same. The two instruments may be in different rooms, but they will be harmoniously together.

Jesus Christ, along with the basic doctrines associated with Him, is our tuning fork. It is often impossible for us to get along with one another but when we each tune our life by His standard the by-product is harmony between us. That is The Emmanuel Factor in relationships.

FUNDAMENTALS

I once asked coach John Wooden, formerly of UCLA, what it takes to make a great basketball team. He, having won more national championships than any other coach, answered rhetorically: "Three things are essential. One, you have to get the team in condition. Two, you have to teach them to play together as a team. Three, you must teach them the fundamentals of the game."

In many churches we spend much time trying "to get the team in condition." We meet, plan, organize, pray, and make sure all the externals are just so. Some churches place emphasis on playing together. Cooperation is basic to success. However, without teaching them the fundamentals we have failed.

The word "fundamental" needs a lot of PR work on

its behalf. It is a negative term which evokes images of extremism. Observation leads some to believe fundamentalists are the most materialistic, success-minded, appearance-obsessed, religious people in America. Unfortunately this description fits some fundamentalists.

However, there are some rational godly people who are intent on communicating "truths once delivered" to faithful people. This they desire to do in a loving manner with academic creditability.

A different connotation of the word is derived from the sports arena and world of music. Vince Lombardi, Tom Landry, Red Auerbach, Dave Brubeck, Bev Shea, and Sandi Patti all have achieved using the fundamentals of their trade. In art, science, and math, fundamentals are respected, and those who have mastered them are admired. If the fundamentals of the Christian faith had not been faithfully propagated, the great spiritual ice age that has chilled the spirit world of Europe would have already made a spiritual Siberia of America.

Liberalism is always a form of erosion, never a tidal wave. Charles Spurgeon astutely observed it and documented it in the British Union. Most ministers in the Union recognized the presence of unbelief within their ranks but assumed it would do no harm. Spurgeon disagreed. He foresaw a future of lifeless and fruitless churches. Early in 1888 he gave a report comparing work of the conservative theological students from his college with that of all other pastors of the Union. During the preceding year 370 college men had baptized 4,770 persons. The increase in their membership amounted to

3,856. The other 1,860 pastors in 2,764 churches reported only 1,770 new members for the year.

In every period of modern church history where a watered-down theology or no theology has been preached, decline has been inevitable. Integrity in message content and messenger character combine to stimulate evangelical and intellectual growth.

Philipp Melanchthon, the intellect behind the Reformation, said:

> In essentials—unity.
> In nonessentials—diversity.
> In all things—love.

Essentials which are considered fundamental to harmony are: The inspiration and infallibility of the Scripture, The Deity of Jesus Christ (including the virgin birth), the substitutionary atonement of Christ's death, the physical bodily resurrection of Christ from the dead, and the literal return of Christ in the second advent.

Each of these is dependent on each preceding one as foundational. If one is disallowed or devalued each is diminished. Many believe these truly enable us to be "joined and knit together." Harmony here is felt to be basic to all else.

> Be conscientious about
> fundamentals,
> but
> not contentious about
> incidentals.

The Emmanuel Factor is the only thing that can bring together and bond together a diverse group honored to be called His "body." Only The Factor can create harmony within diversity. Harmony is a testimony to His presence and His power being at work.

A UNIFIED BODY

These harmoniously together groups called churches have several words applied to them which in part explain their existence. One is *ekklesia*, meaning "called out." Another is *koinonia*, meaning "fellowship." Philologists agree that the root word from which our English word comes, *kuriakon*, means "belonging to a lord." Thus, in these three terms the church is represented as a called-out fellowship belonging to the Lord.

Jesus has deliberately taken upon Himself the building of such a harmonious body. He said, "I will build My church, and the gates of hell shall not prevail against it" (Matt. 16:18).

Properly understood, this statement takes on vibrance. Ancient cities were walled. The elders of the city gathered at the gate of the city to serve as sort of a city council. Here they deliberated the affairs of the city. Jesus in using this expression was saying, "Let the devil and all of his demons get together and confer as to how to stop me, but the collective wisdom of hell can't prevent me from building My church." That suggests all of hell will try to prevent the harmony He proposes. Assurance should be gained from the fact that such collective adversaries can't prevail if His will does avail.

One strategy devised at the gate is dispersion. The German theologian Bultmann coined a phrase for the universal church: "the church without the church." It was a ploy to enlist support for the idea of a universal church without a local church.

Universally the rays of the solar sun are referred to as "the sun." For there to be rays there must be a manifestation of the sun. There must be a sun local for there to be a sun universal. Likewise, for there to be a church universal there must be a church local. Take away the sun local, and there will be no sun universal. Take away the local church, and the church universal ceases to exist.

"New breed" theologian Malcolm Boyd wanted to demolish the "institutional church" and create a more "relevant structure." This too is a "red herring." The expression "red herring" comes from old English law enforcement. When young dogs were being trained a dead herring was dragged across the trail in an attempt to decoy the dog into chasing the wrong thing. Later friends of escapees used this technique to confuse chase dogs. It was a summary term for being misdirected from the primary objective.

The "relevant structure" was an attack on church growth and evangelism. The "church-in-thy-house" philosophy associated with this school of thought was a red herring to divert people from being used of the Lord to build His church. Many are still engaged in the herring chase while they should be engaged in church building.

If diversion won't work to stop the fellowship, enrichment, and expansion called "the church," perhaps dirt will.

Reinhold Niebuhr used an analogy to try to discredit the church. He likened it to Noah's ark, saying that many could not stand the stench in the ark if it were not for the storm outside. Who knows but that Noah and his family were fastidious housekeepers?

There is a "stench" in the church, but undeniably there is a storm outside. One of the most sincere compliments to the worth of an object is trying to copy or counterfeit it. Such attempts are made only in relation to things of value.

Satan has always had his counterfeits in the church. Critics try to pretend this is only a modern phenomenon. A close look at the roles of the New Testament church reveals the thieving Ananias and Sapphira, the profane and vain Hymenaeus and Philetus, Simon who practiced sorcery, and the doctrinally errant and morally corrupt Nicolaitanes.

They also had their genuine lovers of the Lord who willingly paid the price to be used of their Lord in building His church. They together in harmony with Him were an admirable construction crew worthy of our emulation.

They were outmanned and outranked, but they prevailed. An explanation of how is illustrated by an account of a Roman army strategy meeting. The commanding general listened closely as his officers told him of their enemy outnumbering them two to one.

Then he calmly asked, "How many do you count me for?" In assessing your opposition and allies, for how many do you count Christ? This is The Emmanuel Factor that offsets all odds. It is the victory that overcame the world.

NOSEEUMS

If unsuccessful in using the major philosophical strategy, Satan will use the little life-sapping ones. The pioneers who settled western Canada were nearly devoured by tiny gnats called "Noseeums." They were so small as to be almost invisible. Yet, their collective dynamism retarded the conquest of the frontier. Anything Satan can use to disrupt the harmony of Christ's fellowship he will employ, even a noseeum.

C. S. Lewis, the perceptive British writer, astutely noted this. In his captivating work entitled *The Screwtape Letters* he depicts Screwtape (the devil) giving advise to his nephew, Wormwood, his favorite recruiter on earth. He exhorts him: "The church is a fertile field if you just keep them bickering over details, structure, organization, money, property, personal hurts, and misunderstandings . . . One thing you must prevent—don't ever let them look up and see the banners flying, for if they ever see the banners flying you have lost them forever."

When we, individually or collectively, take our eyes off the banners and start looking for noseeums, cacophony, not symphony, results. When The Emmanuel Factor, represented by the banner, is lost sight of, harmony no longer exists.

In a small Tennessee town there is a small church with its name out front on a sign: Left Foot Baptist Church. It was so named years ago when footwashing was in vogue. A great debate erupted in the fellowship over whether to wash the left or right foot first. This group withdrew and named their church after their favorite foot. While looking at feet it is hard to see the banners.

In 1917, the bishops of the Church of Russia held an eventful meeting which resulted in a heated debate. Just down the street a small struggling party of Bolsheviks was plotting an effective, bloody, and ruthless overthrow of the Czar. Their eventual implementation of their plan established their new regime known as the Communist Party. Oh yes, the debate of the bishops—it was an effort to resolve their bitter division over whether to use 18- or 22-inch candles!

It is hard to see the banners when dazzled by noseeums in candlelight.

Let play on the sound track of your mind: "Emmanuel—God with us." Let your retina reflect His banners, the object of your transfixed attention.

A friend of Albert Schweitzer was asked if the doctor ever became discouraged. The answer was "no," and the reason was that he was "so interested in purpose and so concerned with the human potential." For you which will it be, "noseeums" or a clear awareness of The Emmanuel Factor?

LOVE'S STRONG CHORD

Where there is harmony love abides. Recently I stood looking out my hotel window in Topeka, Kansas, at the expansive Topeka State Hospital. As I gazed at the clinic founded by Dr. Karl Menninger I thought of the anguish and suffering alleviated there since the brother team of psychiatrists started it. *The Chicago Daily News* carried a feature story entitled "Love Works Miracles for Mentally Ill in Kansas." The article in part explains the success of the clinic.

"A bit of a miracle in the Kansas flatlands is attracting observers from mental institutions throughout the country. They want to learn the secret of the Topeka State Hospital in returning eight of every ten new patients in the last year to useful lives outside. The secret is not electro-shock, surgery, group therapy, drugs, or any of the conventional treatments of mental disorders. These play a part but the real secret is contained in a single word: love!"

Dr. Karl Menninger further explained: "The doctor doesn't cure by any specific treatment. You cure by atmosphere, by sympathetic understanding on the part of every one in the hospital." He explained further: "By our words and deeds at the hospital, we must gently persuade them that society is worth coming back to. There is none of the professional-staff jealousy that poisons so many institutions. Everyone is on the team. The hospital attendant's opinion is as readily considered as the nurse's or social worker's."

My mind blinked as I turned away from the window view of the clinic, thinking how well that recalled philosophy applies to a church. There love is the fundamental, basic pitch. It must be within a fellowship.

I have never dealt with a person involved in a cult or the occult that did not have the same explanation. In every instance they talk about being accepted, wanted, received, and loved. Never did they talk about being attracted by their teaching. The cult simply made them feel wanted. If these off-the-wall groups are attracting people by love, the church should learn from their experience, if not from the lips of our Lord who commended and commanded love. We too must make people feel loved and wanted. This can only be done where there is genuine love among the body. There can be this warm, attracting love only where there is harmony. The Emmanuel Factor enables this magnetic love.

BONDING UNDER THE BANNER

Jesus Christ said, "No longer do I call you servants . . . but I have called you friends" (John 15:15).

In that same discourse He said, "Greater love has no one than this, than to lay down one's life for his friends" (John 15:13).

In the art gallery of your mind let hang a Scripture portrait of friends. The word "friend" in English, as in its Greek equivalent, *philos*, conveys the idea of loving and being loved.

A London publication gave a prize for the best definition of a *friend*. Some entries were:

"One who multiplies joy and divides grief."
"One who understands our silence."

The winner was: "One who comes in when the world goes out."

One American Indian tribe defined it as "one-who-carries-my-sorrow-on-his-back." What an apt and appropriate definition!

Jesus perfected the art of friendship; and after patterning it, passed it on to us to perform. By His lip and with His life He answered the question: "What is a friend?"

A FRIEND IS COMMITTED

Friendship involves commitment. Christ desires for His followers to be walking examples of His elevated expression: "greater love has no man than this."

Momentary, final embodiment of this declaration by looking into the grey face of death is often easier than slow sacrifice.

> It is as hard at duty's call,
> To lay one's life down day by day,
> As to lay it down once for all.

This requires letting the message of your music become the harmony of your life.

As an insular individual Christ enacted His prophetic utterance: "I lay down my life for you." Today those who love Him honor Him most by obeying His desire as expressed by His friend John: "By this we know love, because He laid down His life for us. And we also ought to lay down our lives for the brethren" (1 John 3:16).

A FRIEND IS COMPLIANT

We are in harmony with Him when we comply with His exortation to "do whatever I command you" (John 15:14).

It is interesting that Jesus said, "You are my friends," not, "I am your friend." For us to say, "Jesus is our friend," is to pull Him down to our level. For Him to say, "You are My friends," is to pick us up to His level.

Friendship involves obedience. Obedience is a loving evidence of togetherness in ideal and intent. Some persons cower at the idea of obedience, thinking it implies subservience. It doesn't. It conveys willful compliance with a heart's wishes.

Epictetus said, "I am free and the friend of God, because I obey Him willingly."

A FRIEND IS COMMUNICATIVE

Of all we need to know Christ said, "I have made known." He has not answered all of our curiosities or explained all of our intellectual probings, but He has told us all we need to know and more than we have evidenced a willingness to obey.

A kindred spirit is essential for harmonious commuication. Those communicate best who have a common heart beating in cadence with Calvary's heart.

A FRIEND IS CHOSEN

Hearts of gratitude should take wings at the thought Christ said, "I have chosen you."

God ". . . chose us in Him before the foundation of the world" (Eph. 1:4).

He chose us! Why? For what purpose?

Joy

Put this on the marquee of your mind: ". . . My joy may remain in you, and that your joy may be full" (v. 11).

A gloomy Christian is a contradiction of terms.

Martin Luther observed: "The devil is a chronic grumbler. The Christian should be a living doxology."

Joy is allied with an invincible host in defense of the glad heart. Joy is a great beautifier, a preserver of youthfulness.

A Hindu asked a native Christian of India, "What medicine do you put on your face to make it shine so?" Responded the Christian, "I don't put anything on it." Certain that he did, the Hindu pressed the point: "Yes, you do. All you Christians do. I've seen shining faces wherever I have met Christians!" Seizing the moment the believer replied: "I will tell you what 'medicine' makes our faces shine—it is the joy in our hearts because Jesus dwells there."

Joy, fresh and cathartic, bubbles to the surface of the face. It causes you frequently to flex your zygomaticus muscles in order to lift the corners of your mouth.

Simultaneously the orbicularis oculi are engaged, causing a slight squint of the eyes. This results in a bright and shining face. Only thirteen muscles are required for a smile. It takes sixty-four facial muscles to frown. Why work so hard? Let joy abound.

Stephen Foster had melancholy thoughts, and his music revealed thoughts of sadness and loneliness. Haydn had bright, cheerful thoughts, and his work pulsated with cheer and joy.

Love

Christ's impassioned appeal to us is to ". . . love one another as I have loved you" (John 15:12).

He has chosen us as objects of His love through which to love an unloving and unlovable world. If we fail to be the conduit through which His love is to flow we further insulate Him from a needy society.

He didn't love us because we were so lovable but because He is so loving. We in turn are to love others as He loved us. He loved us without hesitation, reservation, or qualification. So we are to love in like manner. Gratitude for His love is a great stimulus for loving others.

If we truly love Christ and pure doctrine it is easy to love those who do the same. Conversely, it is our love for Christ and pure doctrine that motivate us to love even those who have absolute disdain for the objects of our love. By maintaining harmony with the heavenly heart we are able to overcome the discordant life. If we love only those who are like us and like us we are no different from those who don't like us. By staying in tune with

Christ we might yet be able to enable those not in harmony with Him to allow Him to fine tune them. For them ever to want such a supernatural tuning they must hear the harps of heaven in our every heartbeat. We must make the Master's melody ring in their consciences. This we must first do by our example.

Hear this verse metered after 1 Corinthians 13: "Though I am a proponent of the doctrine of innerancy and have a Ph.D. in philosophy and psychology; and though I am an authority on social ministries and a master of Brunner; though I speak Hebrew and Greek and use the language of the scientific laboratory so as to dazzle even the elect with my eloquence; if I have not the love of my Lord, the message of my Master, I am no more useful than a singing dog who has lost his voice."

To profess Christ and not practice love is to serve as Satan's decoy, a sinner's alibi, and insulation between Christ and the world He wants to use us to reach. The church is His show case and the redeemed His trophies.

A waiting world echoes the comment of Albert Einstein who said: "If any church would be content to have Jesus' teachings of love as its creed, I would join that church."

Only the secure can love. To love is to make oneself vulnerable. When we open ourselves to others we become as exposed—as exposed as Christ. We must, however, be vulnerable in order to be visible. Our mission is to mirror Christ.

Those whose hearts are in harmony with Christ, who practice His precepts and maintain doctrinal integrity, have reason for relaxed confidence which releases them to love freely. When the strength of the ice is known, the skater can be relaxed and then confidently perform. When the fundamentals are known and accepted the believer can improvise ways of loving others.

Friends

A believer's relationship with Christ reaches a new zenith in Him saying, "I have called you friends" (John 15:15).

This term was used in kingly courts of the Roman Empire. Confidants of the king were called "friends of the king." They ranked in importance above his generals. Access was afforded them to the king as to no others.

Inherent in the meaning of the ancient usage of the term "friend" was the concept of "partner." A slave was defined as "a living tool."

As a child I was fortunate to live in a big house with both a front and back porch. These porches were made of wood. If not kept well painted they would rot. Dad was a talented craftsman. One late summer afternoon I passed as he was painting the porch with a four-inch brush. He called out, "Son, get that other brush and help me so we can finish before dark." Enthusiastically I grabbed what I know now to have been that one-inch brush and dipped deep and brushed hurriedly. To this day just recalling it gives me pride of being a fellow-worker, a partner, with my dad. We did it!

By comparison, our efforts with our divine Companion are even less consequential. However, there is in-

herent in the doing a gratifying and satisfying pride of
His being glorified in our partnership.

Ambassadors

Remember, He said, "you are appointed" (John
15:16).

Our ancestral brothers and sisters in Christ assumed
that assignment with such tenacity that Tertullian writing around the turn of the second century observed in a
communique to the Roman Emperor: "We are but of yesterday and yet already we fill your cities, your islands,
your camps, your palace, your senate, your forum. We
have left you only your empty heathen temple."

What it means to be an ambassador is summarily
contained in the instructions given by Christ to one freed
from demon possession: "Go home to your friends, and
tell them what great things the Lord has done for you,
and how He has had compassion on you" (Mark 5:19).

Finally, He has chosen us as . . .

Advertisements

Christ instructed us to "bear fruit" (John 15:16).
We are not chosen to be pets but patterns.

Life's greatest gesture of friendship is to introduce
your friend to Christ. For this to happen you might well
have to make the introduction by your life-style. Once a
living example inspires a person it is much easier verbally
to share the faith.

Remember, to tune two instruments to each other and for them to play in harmony there must be a basic pitch. By fine tuning your life to that of Christ others will want to join the harmony.

5

God with Us in *Holocaust*

Max Gabriel's "The Last Token" transfixed me. Just being in the Louvre again was exhilarating. Having seen copies and prints I resolved to see the original on this trip to Paris.

Gabriel has depicted the intense drama of the Roman amphitheater during the era of Christian persecution. Captured on his canvas is a beautiful, slender young woman isolated in the arena with an irrepressible wild tiger. Above the restricting stone walls rises tier after tier of seats filled with bloodthirsty spectators made brutish by their sins. The iron gate of the vivarium in which the beasts were caged had been opened. From it has come the tiger enraged by hunger and fear. Confidently the maddened beast creeps from the den with his blood-lusty eyes fixed on his defenseless prey.

Attired in all white except for a dark mantle over her head and shoulders she stands only a few feet from her stalking predator. Her preoccupation isn't with the tiger. She seems impervious to his presence. On the sand before her is a solitary white rose. Obviously it has been thrown there by a relative or lover. Now it becomes apparent why it is the rose and not the taunted tiger that has arrested her attention. Resolutely her upturned and composed gaze is into the crowd. From one of those many rows of seats a special someone had thrown the rose. Her searching eyes scanned the crowd for that one. Inspired by the presence of the source of the rose her spirit had soared above the hate of those who had condemned her to death. She was insensitive to the oncoming ravenous beast that was about to spill her virgin blood and savage her svelte body.

One single rose, "The Last Token," and the loving presence represented thereby changed the entire episode. For the moment there was for her no tiger, no derisive mob, no sand soon to absorb her blood. There was only a rose—and love transcending.

We, like she, are in an inhospitable arena. Society around us is no less a maddened mob intent on letting the blood of the Christian conscience. Persecution for the faith is now more social, political, and economic. It is no less real. In a culture uncharitable to the Christian faith there is a source of inspiration. "The Ultimate Token" of heaven's love graces the arena's floor. It is the Rose of Sharon, Emmanuel, God with us.

Look up, keep the faith, hope abounds! God is with us.

A six-year-old told his buddy: "Mom's in the hospital, and me and Daddy and George and the twins are here all alone." Persons without a personal relationship with Christ can relate to that. No matter who is present, if He is not with you, there is a void. Even a vast web of relationships cannot replace the vacancy caused by the absence of Christ.

Even in the life of a believer, if a tidal wave of cacophonous voices is allowed to subdue the "still small voice" of our beloved Lord, there is a sense of aloneness. Even if we believers feel alone and forsaken we should pause and thank the Lord that He is with us. This superimposition of the will over the emotion will soon bring the emotional state under its sway of assurance. Feelings are fickle, but facts are fixed. The chalk marks on the blackboard of eternity will always read: "Emmanuel."

Just when it seemed He would never leave His disciples He appeared to leave. Just when it seemed He had forsaken them it became apparent He had not.

When you find that parallel in your life remember their renewal and be revived by it. Mirrored in their experience is a pattern found in the Old Testament and repeated in our lives. It is: anticipation followed by frustration followed by realization. The disciples anticipated a "kingdom." The crucifixion resulted in frustration as the kingdom dream vanished. Three days later dawn's early light revealed an empty tomb. Rejoice! The kingdom era was born.

During periods of anticipation and realization it is easy to sense His presence and praise Him. However, the periods of frustration make it appear He is not with us. When the honey of life turns to ashes we need written across the blueprint of our minds: "Emmanuel—God with us."

By Him we are *INDWELT*. Realization that you are indwelt by His supernatural presence gives confidence. Confidence in God gives courage toward all things. Confidence and courage are twins born together who live together in the same heart. Persons who maintain courage amid ridicule, mockery, scoffing, and other forms of persecution are demonstrating confidence in God. Conversely those who lose their courage are evidencing a lack of confidence in God.

By Him we are INSPIRED. The inspiration of a worthy example has motivated many. Ancient Romans kept a bust or painting of their most famous and heroic relative inside the entrance of their homes. It served as a reminder of the noblest and best to enable the youngest and embolden the oldest.

Numerically superior forces of Santa Ana pushed troops of Sam Houston into a perilous position. As though toying with them he paused before the final assault. During that lull the wiley Houston reminded his men how Santa Ana had overrun the Alamo and desecrated the bodies of their comrades by burning them. He concluded by saying: "Remember the Alamo." With that battle cry Houston's ragtag band went against Santa Ana's army, routing and defeating them. They were inspired by a worthy example.

The writer of Hebrews (12:2) appeals to us to accept Jesus as an example of one inspired by that which was worthy: "Looking unto Jesus, the author and finisher of our faith, who for the joy that was set before him endured the cross, despising the shame, and has sat down at the right hand of the throne of God." The joy set before Christ which inspired Him was our salvation. He who inspires us was in His death inspired by us.

By Him we are INCITED. Inspiration must result in action if it is to come to full flower and not die as a bud. Impression without expression can lead to depression. Timorously we might well retreat if we have to engage in spiritual warfare alone. Our standard is: "The measure of the stature of the fullness of Christ" (Eph. 4:13). Holy boldness results in a life preoccupied with Him.

The principle cause of physical heart trouble is the lack of exercise. Americans have more coronaries than any other people. Inactivity is credited as being the principle contributor. In the spiritual realm the same is true. Spiritual inactivity causes spiritual heart trouble. Those who can say with the Psalmist, "I have set the Lord always before me . . ." (16:8), will be flooded with enthusiasm for the work He has allotted. To expose yourself to Him is to expose yourself to enthusiasm. Christ-birthed enthusiasm overcomes lethargy, banishes discouragement, abolishes indifference, and gets things done. It never allows you to sit on your apathy. By the gift of encouragement Christ always brings out the best in everyone. An awareness of His inspiring, indwelling presence rejuvenates the soul and gives an attitude adjustment. By it we are incited to serve actively.

By Him we are INSTRUCTED. Confidently, we can rely on wisdom quoted by the writer of Hebrews, "He has said, 'I will never leave you nor forsake you.' So we may boldly say: 'The Lord is my helper; I will not fear. What can man do to me?'" (Heb. 13:5-6).

From the archives of music lore comes a refreshing account of an experience in the life of Ignace Jan Paderewski. The composer-pianist was scheduled to perform in a major American theater. Elite members of the music-loving community filled the theater for this black-tie affair. Among that prestigious crowd were a mother and her little son. She had taken him hoping the boy might be inspired by the performance to practice his piano lessons. Motherly instincts momentarily lapsed as she engaged in polite conversation with those seated near her. Her little son, a living "squirm machine," could stay seated no longer. Undetected he slipped from his seat and wandered into the aisle. Magnetically he was drawn down toward the platform as others chatted and awaited the performance. Relentlessly he made his way methodically toward the captivating ebony Steinway with its black-and-white keys. Gingerly he sat on the leather-tufted seat, placed his trembling little fingers in just the right place on the keyboard, and began to play. For a moment the house was hushed by the sounds of "Chopsticks." Once it was realized what was happening the irritated, sophisticated audience lost its dignity and began shouting: "Get that boy away from there. Where are his parents? Somebody stop him."

Backstage, Paderewski overheard the melee and instantly surmised what was happening. Hastily he put on his coat and rushed out onstage. Without a word of public announcement he walked up behind the boy, stooped over, reached around both sides of the boy, and began to improvise a countermelody to harmonize with and enhance "Chopsticks." Together they played as Paderewski kept whispering in the child's ear, "Keep going. Don't quit, son. Keep on playing . . . Don't quit . . . Don't stop."

When you are doing your best, and it seems as insignificant as "Chopsticks" to a disapproving world, just listen for the voice of the Master as He improvises on your behalf. Feel the warmth of His loving presence, sense His approval, and hear His whispered instruction, "I will never leave you nor forsake you."

Keep your mind on the rose and your eye on its Source.

Some minds have mountain ridges running through them. Come climb three summits of Romans 5:1-5 to rise above the holocaust.

THE CONDUCT

Christ-pleasing character is seen in the two words "rejoice" and "glory." Both are attitudes. Attitudes are not determined by circumstances but by our thoughts. What happens to us is not as important as our attitude about it and how we react to it.

Victor Frankl, a courageous Jew in Hitler's holocaust, endured indignity and humiliation. He was robbed of his freedom, removed from his family, and relieved of all his possessions, including his watch and wedding ring. His captors shaved his head, stripped him, and stood him in the glaring lights of his interrogators who falsely accused him. Mutely he stood, a helpless pawn in hostile hands. Alone, he had nothing. He said that, as they stripped him of his last possession, his wedding band, it suddenly occurred they had taken the last thing they could take. He had remaining one last thing they could not take—his attitude. He was free to choose his own attitude: bitterness or forgiveness.

Frankl is in no small way like all of us. His was an exaggerated, dramatic likeness to that which we all suffer to some degree. We too must remain mindful there is one thing which only we govern. We are free to choose. We can choose to rejoice or rebel; glory or gripe. Circumstances do not dictate our choice. That alone is ours to make. With Christ as our indwelling, inspiring, and inciting Lord we can but choose the right attitude—gratitude.

The word "rejoice" refers to an overt response to inner peace and happiness. The key word is "inner." It is the outworking response resulting from the indwelling Christ molding our attitude.

Motivating others is not a difficult task. Keeping others from *demotivating* us is a full-time job. Our inner life and outer life are like two liquid solutions separated by a porous membrane. On one side is distilled water, on the other, a salt concentrate. Such an arrangement always results in movement. The movement is inevitably from the solution of greater concentration to that of a lesser concentration.

Which has the greater concentration of influences: your inner life or your outer life? The indwelling Christ wants to work His way through your life out into an environment lacking His presence. This spiritual osmosis enables rejoicing amid adversity.

A further breakdown of the text gives helpful insights. "Rejoice" is in the present tense, meaning to keep on rejoicing. A believer's life-style is to be characterized by rejoicing. At this point many fail miserably. Ask the average Christian: "How are you?" and get ready for an organ recital.

Casual greeting offers an opportunity for rejoicing. A weary world doesn't expect anything but gloom. A positive response reveals an internal, invisible means of support. Anybody can rejoice in the good times. Only an indwelt believer can keep on rejoicing, regardless of circumstances. Adversities are in part allowed by God to give us an opportunity to evidence His sufficiency. A critical or complaining nature betrays Him and discredits His ability to sustain us. As the aroma of something good baking indicates there are goodies in the oven, so a rejoicing heart reveals Christ in the life. To rejoice is to give credit to Him; to respond negatively is to discredit Him. You and you alone choose which.

"Rejoice" is in the middle voice, meaning the subject, *you*, benefits. Clinically this is now substantiated. A spirit of rejoicing results in the body releasing endorphins and enkephalins which are natural, made in the body, neurotransmitters. The word "endorphin" comes from (end)ogenous and m(orphin)e. The word "enkephalin" comes from the Greek roots for "inside the head." They perform morphine-like activities. This wholesome type of natural morphine is calming, restoring, and pain-reducing. Properly produced by natural bodily processes they are basically harmless and can be addictive. Indirectly that means rejoicing can be addictive, habit-forming. The more you rejoice the more of these two pentapeptides your body produces. With your body producing more there is a greater natural tendency for the body to want more. Instinctively your body is begging you to rejoice and provide more of these health aids. Chemically and spiritually a person who rejoices tends to keep rejoicing.

Think of it: *you*, the subject, benefits. Keep on rejoicing to keep on benefiting.

A clinical study done by Duke University Medical Center shows that being negative, cynical, and complaining is unhealthy. Persons of such temperaments have five times more heart disease than others. Further definition reveals that certain types of hostility, mistrust, and bitterness are even more significant factors. Such attitudes are not only detrimental to physical health but destructive of spiritual vitality.

You also benefit spiritually. Anytime there is a sense of having pleased the Lord there is satisfaction. He has by precept and practice established the fact He wants His people to rejoice. To do so is to glorify Him and gratify yourself.

"We won! We won!" she kept saying, jumping up and down. The excitement of this little cheerleader was contagious. The football team representing her school had just defeated their biggest rival. Jubilantly she continued, "We won!" What an editorial "we." She didn't have on a football uniform and hadn't been on the field, yet she was insistent that "we" had won.

Hers was victory by association. Those representing her had triumphed. This proxy victory was no less hers, however. By identifying with those who actually paid the physical price of victory she was a victor.

When we identify with the victorious, indwelling Christ we too can rejoice knowing "we won." The little cheerleader's feelings and conditions became secondary. Her associated-victory was what motivated her. When we intimately identify with the victory once and for all won by Christ, that influences our outlook, regardless of the day's outcome. With Christ as our supernatural teammate we are perpetual winners.

It is difficult to determine the outcome of a war from the viewpoint of one soldier. That is, unless that soldier is the commanding officer. From our individual perspective it is difficult to assess the true result of our daily combat. Together with Him we triumph all the way. To rejoice always we must develop this associated-victory mentality.

When fresh winds of newness stop blowing and the aroma of staleness prevails, let one name vibrate the innermost strings of the harp of your heart: Emmanuel. Rejoice! In Him we won and that makes us winners.

"Rejoice" is hortatory, meaning it perpetually carries the weight of a command. Do it! Though to the wondering world it is an alternative life-style, it is not for the Christian an option. To remain obedient we must do it.

The personal pleasure of pleasing another is wrapped up in doing it. When circumstances suggest no reason for rejoicing, and yet we rejoice, we then have reason to rejoice. Rejoice that He gives you reason and capacity to rejoice.

We are not only to "rejoice" but also to "glory" (5:3). This word means to "exalt" even in the midst of adversity. Once justified we have no reason for personal boasting. Once justified we have continual reason to "glory" forever. That is, we have reason to speak with high exaltation in the sphere within which we live with Christ. We have reason in all adversity to glory in our Mediator Christ and on the eternal Word of promise. We need not wait for conditions to change and improve because He and His Word never change with conditions. He is the fulcrum of our faith. He lifts us, enabling us to glory.

THE CONDITION

According to the inspired penman we are to glory "in tribulations." This expression means "in the midst of and because of our suffering." In our own holocaust we are to glory.

But how?

Burn this on the pages of your mind: Your needs are a vestibule of His presence.

Let your mind marinate in this: "My grace is sufficient for you, for my power is made perfect in weakness" (2 Cor. 12:9).

We Christians must be like pokeweed: When cut low we just come back stronger!

Adversity becomes an avenue of acclaim when you know your own weakness. By contrast it serves to magnify His strength. Your suffering is His opportunity. Only you can keep Him from using it for your good and His glory. You can do it by the attitude you manifest.

Only when we in our suffering realize we are weak and He is strong, able, and ready to aid us do we seek help from Him. In doing so we find it. In finding it we have reason to glory in Him. What occasioned this glorying? Adversity. Rather, His presence with us in adversity.

The word translated "tribulation" means adversity and pressure. As there is pop art so there is pop Christianity. Currently the "immune syndrome" is vogue. That is, God wants you healthy, wealthy, and carefree. However, the Bible at no point promises exemption from adversity or immunity from problems. He does promise to be with us in them and give victory over them. There is no elevated stage of spirituality which when achieved will guarantee no more problems. That mentality has caused much frustration among some of God's most loyal subjects. This pseudo-school of thought implies that any problem is a revelation of a flaw in your relationship with the Lord. It is actually an opportunity for you to demonstrate just how good the Lord really is.

I visited my friend Bill Westbrook in Veterans Hospital. He was there for operation number thirty-two. This saintly servant of our Lord lived totally for Him. Such a life-style had not kept him from tribulation.

Upon greeting him I asked, "How are you?" His response was as close to a negative as I have ever gotten from him. He answered, "Well, Pastor, yesterday I got down a bit. You know I don't ever want to indicate I am discouraged with the Lord." Then as he reached over and picked up his New Testament, he continued, "When I got to feeling a little low I just got 'the Word' and the Lord and I worked it out."

That is exhibit A of what it means to "glory in tribulation."

THE CONSEQUENCE

If we rejoice and glory in tribulation there are natural consequences.

It results in our "knowing" certain principles. Knowing is a reference to inherent knowledge of God's promises and provisions. Experience will prove Him faithful.

One thing known is that tribulation "produces" certain things. The word translated "produces" or "worketh" refers to something inside working its way out. When you have inherent academic facts and experiential knowledge within, they inevitably work their way out. A bubble in a liquid can't be suppressed; it will inexorably work its way to the top. An awareness of the indwelling Christ works itself out, enabling the believer to rejoice and glory in adversity.

One form in which it bubbles to the surface is in "patience" or "perseverance." This does not mean passive indifference but rather active consistency in pursuit of purpose.

Phillips Brooks, the former New England pulpiteer, was known for his calm demeanor. Like most persons he was also known by his intimates to have moments of anxiety. One day as he paced the floor a friend asked, "What is the trouble, Dr. Brooks?" He responded, "The trouble is that I am in a hurry, but God isn't."

When you feel that way, and most of us do, guess whose clock needs to be reset!

Andrew Murray, once given occasion to practice what he preached, wrote: "Be assured that, if God waits longer than you could wish, it is only to make the blessing doubly precious! God waited four thousand years, till the fullness of time, ere He sent His Son. Our times are in His hands; He will avenge His elect speedily; He will make haste for our help, and not delay one hour too long!"

Patience gives birth to character. This "experience" refers to being tested to see if you are ready for a blessing. It staggers the imagination to think of the blessing we might have missed because of tests we have failed. When next trapped in an adversity let your responsive reaction be governed by imagining what blessing the Lord has already loaded on His divine delivery truck. Then resolve to act in such a way that it won't have to be put back in His warehouse or given to someone else. By recognizing adversity as an advantage, hope springs up.

The word "hope" refers to happy anticipation of future certainty. Time between the receiving of a promise and its fulfillment is spanned by hope. It is the assurance that what is promised will be delivered and thus reacting accordingly.

Upon completing taking a roll of film one might say, "I hope they turn out good." Having used the proper film in a good camera with all the right settings you can have happy anticipation of their development. This is hope in photography and in all phases of life.

"This hope we have as an anchor of the soul, both sure and steadfast . . ." (Heb. 6:19). Sailors can't see their anchor once it is lowered in the water. Knowing its capacity gives them hope in their mooring. Like an anchor, hope enables us to ride out life's storms confidently.

Abraham is a model of hope enacted. Abraham and his wife Sarah had long since passed their childbearing years when they received a special promise for God. On the basis of His own integrity God promised them a son. Physiologically there was no possibility that this could happen. Yet, "In hope against hope he believed . . ." (Rom. 4:18). That means simply it didn't make sense. With no faith in his own body but great faith in the Lord the character of Abraham showed itself. Therefore, ". . . not being weak in faith, he did not consider his own body, already dead (since he was about a hundred years old) and the deadness of Sarah's womb. He did not waver at the promise of God through unbelief, but was strengthened in faith, giving glory to God and being fully convinced that what He had promised He was able to perform" (Rom. 4:19-21).

While awaiting the future certainty with happy anticipation Abraham went about giving glory to the Lord. That's hope.

Hope has to have an object if it is to be sustained. Our hope must be Christocentric. Paul reminded Timothy of this when he wrote of "Jesus Christ our hope" (1 Tim. 1:1). Our hope is not reliant upon some plan, program, or even a panacea, but on a person, a person with us, Emmanuel.

Now come back to the Roman arena in contemporary reality. As you enter note the podium, Caesar's seat, is still identified. To your left is the Porta Sanavivaria, the door of health and life. To your right the Porta Libertina, the door of the goddess of corpses, through which fallen warriors or slain martyrs were dragged.

On the floor of the arena is the equivalent of a rose, "The Last Tribute." It is a cross which was first erected there in 1300 as a memorial to the Christian martyrs. At the base of the cross in Latin is inscribed: "Ave crux spes unica," that is, "Hail to thee, O Cross, the only hope!"

Look up. Fix your eyes, not upon the tiger of tribulation, but look full on His wonderful face. The cross declares that love transcends.

6

God with Us in *Heartache*

At an enjoyable dinner Johnny Cash told me the following first-person story.

"It was a big night. They had asked me to do a benefit performance for a worthy charity. The former first lady, Mamie Eisenhower, was the Honorary Chairlady.

"Preliminary events had wound down, and it was now my moment onstage. It being a very special event I had a new black suit made for it. This was a sharp tailor-made outfit with lots of spangly, dangly things on it. The pants were skintight.

"After the fanfare the curtain opened, and there I stood at center stage in the spots. Before I hit my first lick on my guitar I dropped my pick. Without thinking I stooped to pick it up. As I did I heard something rip. Looking down I saw my pants leg seam had ripped from the knee to the crotch. As I looked up, there sat Mamie on the front row looking like she hadn't seen anything. I straightened up and struggled through my first number.

"As soon as I finished I rushed offstage to my dressing room. June followed me. I slammed the door and be-

gan stripping off that outfit. I threw it on the floor and
began jumping up and down on it. I screamed and yelled
like a spoiled brat. All the while June was cowered in a
corner. Suddenly she burst out laughing. I said, 'What's
the matter with you, woman?' She said, 'Johnny, this is
the funniest thing I have ever seen.' 'Funny,' I said,
'what's so funny?'

"Attempting to catch her breath she said, 'Johnny,
you have the number-one song on the charts in "A Boy
Named Sue." You just made a movie in which you star.
You even have your own TV program—and God done
busted yore britches!'"

Has God ever "busted yore britches?"

He did Paul's. He related his story in 2 Corinthians
12. After telling of his exhilarating experiences of being
caught up into the third heaven, a truly "heady" happening, he wrote of his humiliation:

> And lest I should be exalted above measure
> by the abundance of the revelations, a thorn in
> the flesh was given me, a messenger of Satan to
> buffet me, lest I be exalted above measure.
> Concerning this thing I pleaded with the Lord
> three times that it might depart from me. And
> He said to me, "My grace is sufficient for you,
> for My strength is made perfect in weakness."
> Therefore most gladly I will rather boast in my
> infirmities, that the power of Christ may rest
> upon me. (vv. 7-9).

Paul's deepest humiliation, a "thorn in the flesh,"

and his highest exaltation, "visions and revelations of the Lord," were linked. This is an often-repeated pattern in every life. It was in Christ's. His baptism, a moment of exaltation, was followed by the temptations in the wilderness, a time of humiliation. When on either curb of life's roller coaster we can always be aware of the other and how it helps serve as a balancing factor in life. We must not make the mistake of thinking either is permanent.

Life, if likened to a chemical situation, is not a mixture of exaltation and humiliation but rather a compound. If sulphur and iron filings are mixed, they can be separated by a magnet. If the two are mixed and heated they melt together and become one, a compound, ferrous sulfide. Together our exaltation and humiliation form a compound intended to conform us to the image of Christ.

Paul noted three factors in his experience that helped form such a compound. In each instance he spoke of a *source* and a *solution*.

AN EXTERNAL FACTOR

Summarily Paul spoke descriptively of something in his life as "a thorn in the flesh." God exercised heavenly wisdom in not identifying the thorn. To have identified it would have made the account of less value to those who could not identify with it specifically. Naming it would have made his experience remote to all but a few.

Speculation is varied and wide including such things as embarrassing baldness, being a hunchback, poor vision, sensual passion, epilepsy, headaches, or malaria. When I ventilate my imagination and speculate I add Alexander the coppersmith whom Paul described as one who "did me much harm" (2 Tim. 4:14). Again conjecture suggests Alexander might have been an old friend from the past who was not a believer. Knowing Paul's past he followed him around, trying to discredit him and his witness by recounting the apostle's sordid past. For those who have such a nemesis such random thought gives courage, but to all others it discounts the true value of an unidentified thorn.

The "thorn" is to all a symbol of some perpetual perplexity, a constant cause of consternation. Everybody can relate to that. Don't be overly concerned about what his thorn was. Just work at applying his solution to your situation.

Source

God provides no wall to shield us from all harm. He does provide His grace as a transforming perimeter. Thus, any assault from the enemy coming through His shield of grace is transformed into that which can produce a good result.

Whatever the thorn was, Paul said it did "buffet me." The word "buffet" was descriptive of striking one with the fist. Psychologically, emotionally, and spiritually, if not physically, Paul was being beaten black and blue. The word "buffet" is in the present tense, indicating it was not a single, isolated trial, but continual. Its chronic nature made it more critical.

Persons in such a state can relate to what God offered Paul. We, as he, prefer immunity, desire exemption, seek relief, and strive for escape. Such conduct is natural. That, however, is often part of the problem. The solution is frequently not natural but supernatural.

The tests He allows you are His vote of confidence in you.

There is a near cultic concept moving throughout Christendom today variously called "Atonement Healing" or "Healing on Demand." It has as its thesis that God's children in His will enjoy only health and good fortune. Correctly applied the Bible does not teach this. Many conscientious Christians, who are living with all their being a godly life, do suffer. Exposure to this false teaching frustrates many of them. Living for the Lord and still having problems, they assume they are failing Him and try even harder to please Him. When the problem doesn't go away they suffer mental anguish.

Sickness and suffering are various forms of buffeting. From where do they come? Four basic sources need to be considered.

(a) *Sometimes they come from God.* He warned His people of this in Deuteronomy 28:58-59: "If you do not carefully observe all the words of this law that are written in this book, that you may fear this glorious and awesome name, THE LORD YOUR GOD, then the Lord will bring upon you and your descendants extraordinary plagues—great and prolonged plagues—and serious and prolonged sickness."

Herod's plight for disobedience is graphically spoken of in Acts 12:23: "Then immediately an angel of the Lord struck him, because he did not give glory to God. And he was eaten by worms and died." The worms were not a consequence of his death but the cause of it.

Why does God ever perpetuate such things? For one of two reasons: discipline or an occasion for witness. His wisdom and love are both involved in determining when such should be allowed.

In the victorious roll call of faith found in Hebrews 11, a number of persons are noted as having experienced great victories through faith. Then in concluding the chapter several examples are cited of persons with faith just as strong who had a different result:

> And others were tortured, not accepting deliverance, that they might obtain a better resurrection. Still others had trial of mockings and scourgings, yes, and of chains and imprisonment. They were stoned, they were sawn in two, were tempted, wandered about in goatskins, being destitute, afflicted, tormented—of whom the world was not worthy . . . and all these, having obtained good testimony through faith . . . (Heb. 11:35-39).

It was not a lack of faith that caused their "thorns." Their thorns were an occasion for a positive witness. Their epitaph might well have been "of whom the world was not worthy."

(b) *Sometimes they come from the devil.* Satan and sin can cause suffering according to Luke 13:11,16. Satan had the woman spoken of bound by "a spirit of infirmity eighteen years." James 5 also connects sin and sickness.

The author of Acts (10:38) wrote of "how God anointed Jesus of Nazareth with the Holy Ghost and with power; who went about doing good, and healing all that were oppressed of the devil; for God was with Him."

(c) *A third cause is one's own personal life-style.* Bodily abuse has a natural consequence. The results of 6,000+ calories a day can't be blamed on God or Satan. The consequence of smoking two packs a day can't be laid off on God or the devil. Deferred payment causes many willingly to abuse their body today for the pleasure involved, knowing that payment won't have to be made for a few years. Be kind to your tomorrow self. Don't overly indulge your body today because there are natural consequences to be faced in the future.

Those who don't eat right, rest right, work right, and sleep right must eventually pay for their intemperance.

(d) Another cause is simply the failing flesh of our human nature. There are certain natural laws at work which affect adversely human life. As members of a fallen race there is a price to be paid. Sometimes the innocent suffer with the guilty. If a would-be parent indulges in non-prescription drugs a child conceived may suffer malformation, retardation, or addiction as a result. God can't be blamed for natural consequences.

Rather than spend time analyzing the cause of every "thorn," why not study how it can be used constructively? Don't dwell on the cause but the consequence. Instead of concentrating on the physical effect, think of the spiritual significance.

Solution

The solution for dealing with external sources is the *WISDOM* of God. Concerning the visions and revelations primarily, but regarding the entire matter in general, Paul said, "God knows." As a child, that thought frightened me. The idea that God was watching caused me to tremble, knowing He was aware of my every failure. However, it soon occurred to me that if He were always watching, He also knew when I was in trouble and needed help. That idea is still encouraging. He knows our every need. Knowing this gives cause for confidence.

Though there are times we are insensitive to Him, there is never a time He is unmindful of us. God sees to it that those who want to serve Him are not overrun by strange miseries, sad hours, and bitter disappointments. In His pity He shows us what our distress really means and releases the blessing inherent in it. No violence, not even the wildest tumult, can separate the believer from His love. Many often look back on their greatest anguish and worst perplexity as the very time He did the most for them. Hours of adversity are often the first guided steps on the path of peace, the awakening of a higher value of life, and a clearer light on His will.

Three times Paul prayed for the thorn to be removed. It wasn't. God's answer to our petitions, as here, is often NO with the result being something better. His no's are always positive answers. We need to spend more time thanking Him for the "no" answers. By them He has often kept us from our own worst end and kept us for a better purpose.

Should we expect immunity which not even Christ received? He "who, in the days of His flesh, when He had offered up prayers and supplications, with vehement cries and tears to Him, who was able to save Him from death, and was heard because of His godly fear, though He was a Son, yet He learned obedience by the things which He suffered" (Hebrews 5:7-8).

This clearly says God the Father "was able to save Him from death." Yet He didn't, even with Christ offering an impassioned prayer in Gethsemane. The Father didn't spare the Son in order that He might deliver us. This was the better result. Often His delays, as well as declines, are for a better reason. Our disappointments are often God's appointments.

Christ acquiesced to the will of the Father and prayed, "They will be done . . ." In effect He was saying with Paul, "God knows."

Just when it appeared Satan was about to win a victory it became apparent that the Father had not forsaken the Son. He delivered Him bodily from the grave and thus won the victory. This pattern of victory growing out of the grave of defeat is often repeated in our lives.

We would do well to use prayer in confronting our perplexities as did Paul. Likewise, James gave specific instructions as to what to do in case of sickness. He said, "Is anyone among you sick? Let him call for the elders of the church, and let them pray over him, anointing him with oil in the name of the Lord" (James 5:15). This verse is subject to much misuse and abuse.

First, we misunderstand anointing. Two Greek words are translated anoint. One is *chriō*. It referred to sacred and symbolic use such as in anointing a prophet, priest, or king. It is the root word for "Christ" which means "the anointed one." It involved placing oil on the brow. The other word was *aleiphō* and meant to knead or massage into the body. In the Bible lands, historically and contemporarily olive oil has medicinal connotations. Ancient rabbinical writings spoke of its medical value. In effect, olive oil was considered one of the best medicines of the day. In using *aleiphō* James was saying, "Use the very best medicine available."

Use of medicine is biblical. Jesus implied it when He said, "They that are whole need not a physician, but they that are sick . . ." The Samaritan used olive oil and wine to treat the roadside victim. In the Revelation the Laodicean church was depicted by the expression, "anoint thine eyes."

Christians should always seek the best medical assistance available when a need exists.

Knowing this to be the meaning of the exhortation of James, some, in avoiding the mistaken practice of dabbing oil on the brow, have failed to call people together in prayer for the sick. We as Paul should pray about our "thorns" with trust in God's loving wisdom.

After having used the best medicine available and

having concentrated prayer, we have done all Scripture instructs. Then knowing we have done all Scripture requires we should trust the Lord to do what is best for us.

With confidence like that of ancient Job we should say of God's wisdom: "He knows the way that I take; When He has tested me, I shall come forth as gold" (Job 23:10).

AN INTERNAL FACTOR

Like a pendulum, attitudes swing between arrogant pride and constructive humility. In love our Lord wants to enable us to keep ourselves in check.

Every time there is a listing or a grouping of sins in the Bible the same one always appears first. It is pride. This is the negative form of pride. Ego flights, grandiose self-illusions, or egomania have no place in the life of a believer. There is a positive kind of pride which is constructive. It is the kind which makes persons ashamed not to be or do their best. It is a commendable catalyst in life. False pride is never good.

Paul confessed to the potential of improper pride in his life as a result of the elevated, unique experience of being caught up into the third heaven. There are three heavens spoken of in Scripture. One is the atmosphere in which we live. Above it is the solar heaven occupied by the sun, moon, stars, and planets. The "third heaven" is a reference to God's abode. It is also called "paradise" (2 Cor. 12:4). Paul had visited this place where God abides, where the dead in Christ await resurrection. No other living person could make that statement. This put him in celebrity status. As a center of attention Paul was catered to and sought after by many people.

The Source

To prevent Paul from having an ego-flight, the Lord gave him a "thorn in the flesh" to keep him humble. Whatever it was caused Paul to experience brokenness. Instead of elevation he experienced humiliation resulting in a contrite spirit. This is done in our lives "that we should not trust in ourselves but in God (1 Cor. 1:9). It is to redirect us to the Lord in order that by us others might be attracted to Him by an evidence of his sufficiency.

Our proper humility is aided by a truth Paul earlier penned in challenging the Corinthian church. He wrote: "For who makes you differ from another? And what do you have that you did not receive? Now if you did indeed receive it, why do you glory as if you had not received it?" (1 Cor. 4:7).

True humility can be evidenced by:

- Not praising yourself (Prov. 27:2).
- Serving the undeserving (Matt. 20:26).
- Not choosing the place of prominence (Luke 14:10).
- Submitting ourselves to our elders (1 Pet. 5:5-6).

All four traits were self-evident in Paul's life as a result of the "thorn."

In our achievement-oriented society, ego is encouraged; pride is promoted. Ego-bolstering labels, brands, models, and fads are often sacrificially sought. Many have a maddening drive for recognition, resulting in flattery.

In light of this mania it is difficult to realize the value in not having or not achieving. Society's mentality causes difficulty in realizing what might be achieved by not being able to excel, enjoy the best, or be the best-looking. A paradox results. It is difficult to find contentment while experiencing the things that enable humility. It is hard to limit your prayer to your "daily bread" when the world pushes you to seek to own a chain of bakeries. Our lust for prestige, prominence, publicity, and power is inflamed. This generation might well be described by this statement: "More is better *but* more is never good enough."

We are admonished to "be content with such things as you have. For He Himself has said, 'I will never leave you nor forsake you.' So we may boldly say: 'The Lord is my helper; I will not fear. What can man do to me?'" (Heb. 13:5,6).

Sometimes "such things as you have" are good—sometimes bad. In either instance contentment is encouraged. In the final analysis, true contentment in either condition comes only from relying on the Lord. If He sends the good it is for our good. If He allows the "thorn" it is for our good. Therefore, why fight the good?

John Chrysostom who lived in the fourth century wrote of the blessings inherent in a believer's low estate:

How great is the advantage of affliction;
for now indeed that we are in the enjoyment of
peace we have become supine and lax, and
have filled the Church with countless evils; but
when we were persecuted we were more sober-
minded and more earnest and more ready for
church attendance and for hearing.

The Solution

The solution to this internal state of being brought
low is the *Word* of God. Paul's victory is summed up in
the statement, "And He said to me . . ." (1 Cor. 12:9).

Every prayer has two parts: petition and desire.
Paul's petition was for the thorn to be removed. His desire was to glorify God. The Lord said "no" to the petition and "yes" to the desire. Only by saying "no" to the
former could He say "yes" to the latter. By analyzing
your prayers you might find God has often said "yes" to
your desire without saying "yes" to your petition.

Note what God did say: "My grace is sufficient for
you . . ."

This was a heavenly harmony to silence earth's dis-
cord.

As the "thorn" was a gift so was grace. Those who
have "thorns" can expect grace. Grace is the spiritual
"rose" accompanying "thorns."

In His Word the Lord has revealed many of the secrets of His grace. He has shared more than we have ca-

pacity to absorb, and yet there is more. The secrets God has kept are as good or better than those He has revealed.

Seeing a "thorn" removed is not nearly as glorifying to the Lord as seeing its purpose fulfilled. God always has enough grace to make us "more than conquerors" (Rom. 8:35-37).

"Grace" is God giving to us everything we need or that He asks from us without our deserving it. That little personal pronoun "my" associated with grace makes a heavenly difference. The God who created the galaxies has offered His grace. The God who conquered Canaan against all odds is on your side. The God who opened a sealed tomb and released "the Life" wants to aid your life.

His grace "is" sufficient for you. That being in the perpetual present tense doesn't mean it was or shall be but at any given moment *is* sufficient. It can't be stored and neither can it be depleted. Someone asked a child why he didn't pray for tomorrow's bread also. Replied the child, "Because I don't want stale bread." God's grace never gets stale. He never gives it until needed. He always gives it when needed.

His grace is "sufficient." No matter how severe or how long-lasting the "thorn" God's grace will suffice. There is no need which His supply does not exceed.

For your good and His glory God wants to manifest His grace in your life. As the *shekinah* glory of God on the mercy seat in the tabernacle revealed God's presence, so God's grace in the believer does the same. Open yourself to His grace by submitting to His will.

AN ETERNAL FACTOR

The Source

The Lord God allowed Satan to "buffet" Paul by putting in his life a "thorn" which was "a messenger of Satan." Paul never came to feel that the "thorn" itself was a good thing. He did come to see how God's grace could transform a bad thing into a good use. The "thorn" was not of God, even though it did its work for God.

As in the life of Job, so in the life of Paul, Satan worked within the permissive will of God. He does the same in our lives. The result was not Satan's intent though it was God's purpose. It was to show the sufficiency of His grace. Anyone can brag about the capacity of a doctor. It is only when a patient submits to the diagnosis and treatment of a doctor that the patient proves he truly trusts the doctor's ability. Theoretically anyone can speak of God's grace. When it becomes a personal testimony people listen.

The Solution

The solution was to do the *WORK* of God. Once Paul understood the grace of God He was willing to submit to doing the work of God "most gladly." At that moment he exhibited his enthusiastic eagerness for the will of God. He intimidated the "thorn" by welcoming it. His intent at the moment was to let the "thorn" achieve the Father's will and not Satan's purpose. Extremities caused by the "thorn" gave God the opportunity to demonstrate the sufficiency of His grace. When we grow to interpret our adversities in this light we will have greater peace, and God will be given greater praise. No human adequacy can ever reveal the grace of God like abject weakness.

I have applauded the feats of strength performed by Paul Anderson, long considered the strongest man in the world. Having been in his presence when he lifted over one ton of weight I marveled at his strength. I, as millions, have been blessed by his testimony of his strength being for the glory of God. However, Paul has never been a greater blessing than the times I visited his hospital room after he had two artificial hip implants. There in his pain and weakness he spoke of God's grace. Grimacing in pain and struggling for breath he praised the Lord and spoke of His goodness. It is little wonder that a nurse who attended him said, "Mr. Anderson taught all of us in this hospital some important lessons." By his conduct and conversation he evidenced the sufficiency of God's grace.

Certain strengths often contribute to spiritual weakness. Of King Uzziah it was said: ". . . when he was strong his heart was lifted up, to his destruction, for he transgressed against the Lord his God . . ." (2 Chron. 26:16). God's blessings on him resulted in his becoming arrogant over what he received rather than reliant on the giver. When a blessing gets more attention than the Blessor, then the blessing becomes a spiritual liability.

Paul inventoried some of his "infirmities," that is, weaknesses: "reproaches"—a reference to insults.

"needs"—a summary for hardships.

"persecutions"—a glossary for suppression.

"distresses"—a generality for all difficulties.

Can you relate? God can relate His grace.

We each need to develop a weakness/power complex. That is, we need to become aware of God's power in our time of weakness. As we recognize our times of weakness as opportunities for His power to be manifested, then we will have correctly interpreted them. Only then can we patiently allow His grace to work.

Whether we stand in all our exalted glory on center stage amid the spotlight's glare or humbly stoop with "busted britches," God is still God. His grace is always sufficient. Remember that the next time you hear a rip— or feel the prick of a "thorn."

Always? Always!

7

God with Us in *Holiness*

Sandy was her name though her raven-black hair belied it. I watched her grow from adolescence into young womanhood. Her features were sharp and well-defined, those of an uncommon beauty. Her teenage peers said she was put together by a jeweler because she had "all the right movements."

She grew up in the church. It was the center of her young life. That, though good, isn't good enough. Almost imperceptibly she evolved out of the church scene. Upon leaving for college I lost track of her for a while. The radiance of her smile and warmth of her personality were missed. For the longest no one heard from her after her family moved from our community in New Orleans. A few years lapsed, and a new Sandy reappeared in the Crescent City. She had come back to be the only female Playboy Club manager in America. At a youthful age she had reached the pinnacle of her chosen profession.

This is the rest of the story—the kind *Playboy* never tells. Months later she was on a return flight to "The City Care Forgot." Her seatmate was a long-time friend of mine. Finding that she had grown up in our community he asked if she knew me. At first her look of surprise faded into a pensive expression as the conversation continued. His sharing the love of Christ with her resurrected the Bible truths that had been planted in her youthful mind years before. As he pressed the claims of Christ, all of those seeds sprouted, and she happily gave her heart to Christ.

She tells what happened then. After arriving back at the club, she pulled out a little New Testament given her by our church upon completion of high school. She started reading. Her reverie was interrupted by a sudden presence. Her floor manager "bunny" had come into her office. They being close friends, she began to share what had happened to her. This girl too had a similar background which resulted in the two of them getting down on their knees in the office and committing their lives to Christ.

After the prayer, Sandy picked up the phone to call her friend Hugh Hefner. She told him about Christ saving her, and she resigned her position. The two then changed from their bunny outfits, went out in the club, and began sharing Christ from table to table.

She left the club and city and went back to her parents' home in West Texas—a new creature in Christ.

The Emmanuel Factor was at work in her, manifesting itself in a manner called personal holiness. With it Sandy had the potential of long-sought-for happiness. I am pleased to say she now enjoys it by living for Christ.

God is not overly concerned about your happiness,

but He does have a depth of concern about your holiness. He wants you to be holy because He knows that only then can you be happy. Had Sandy stayed in her old environment her new nature would have made her "out of sync" with the old. A lack of harmony between her heart and habitat would have made happiness impossible.

Jesus said, "Blessed are those who hunger and thirst after righteousness, For they shall be filled" (Matt. 5:6). The filling, the happiness, comes only after the hunger and thirst for righteousness have been satisfied and quenched by holiness. Happy is the person whose most intense desire is to enter into and maintain a right relationship with God. This relationship comes through regeneration and consequents in reformation. Doctrine and duty, belief and behavior, concepts and conduct, relationship and responsibility are all linked.

Charles Wesley posed a question and then answered it, "What is our calling, our glorious hope, but inward holiness?"

Holiness, rightly comprehended, is an admirable and attractive attribute in a life. Those who are holy are not persons with a halo and an aura of ethereal remoteness. They are easily lovable people with a sparkle in their eyes, a spring in their steps, and a note of joy in their voices. Holiness, though practical and practicable, has been distorted in modern minds. Gaunt, reclusive hermits are envisioned by many when they think of holy men. Unapproachable, condemning, solitary persons with stained glass in the tone of their voices often come to mind. To be holy doesn't mean to sit around in a fetal position eating lettuce leaves and birdseed while contemplating your navel. Such an image is foreboding and forbidding.

Thank God these are improper images. Whatever else a holy person is, he or she should be functional, graceful, and appealing. When Sandy gave her life to Christ she did not give up any of her wit, wisdom, beauty, or charm. To be holy doesn't mean to abdicate your intellect, abort your personality, or abandon your sense of humor. These and all other attributes and assets are merely brought under Christ's control for a life to be holy.

Charles H. Spurgeon, the prince of the nineteenth-century pulpit, described holy persons properly when he wrote,

> It would be a great pity if in the process of being qualified for the next life, we became disqualified for this; but it is not so. It would be a very strange thing if, in order to be fit for the company of angels, we should grow unfit to associate with men; but it is not so. It would be a singular circumstance if those who speak of heaven have nothing to say concerning the way thither; but it is not so. . . . True religion has as much to do with this world as with the world to come; it is always urging us onward to the higher and better life; but it does so by processes and precepts which fit us worthily to spend our days while here below.

At the moment you put your faith in Christ there is a creative transferral that transpires. Your guilt is transferred to Christ, and His spiritual nature becomes your new-life principle. Paul described it this way. "I have been crucified with Christ; it is no longer I who lives, but Christ lives in me; and the life which I now live in the flesh I live by faith in the Son of God, who loved me and gave Himself for me" (Gal. 2:20).

For holiness to prevail and to produce happiness there must be posted on the wall of the mind a happy "no longer I" sign read and responded to consistently. When we identify with Christ in His death, He identifies with us in our life. His holiness which impacts our life must be imparted to the world.

Dr. A. J. Gordon wrote:

The men who conquered the Roman Empire for Christ bore the aspect of invaders from another world, who absolutely refused to be naturalized to this world. Their conduct filled their heathen neighbors with the strangest perplexity; they were so careless of life, so careful for conscience, so prodigal of their own blood, so confident of the overcoming blood of the Lamb, so unsubdued to the customs of the country in which they sojourned, so mindful of the manners of that country from which they came not.

Christ is looking for people like that today. He is not scouting merely for people with ability but people of faith; people who refuse to doubt; people who simply believe Christ is not merely sufficient, but superior.

Tertullian wrote of the spiritual warfare descriptively when he reported, "We engage in these conflicts as men whose very lives are not their own." He and his colleagues had consigned their wills to Christ and with Paul could say, "I have been crucified with Christ."

Such holiness is possible because, as Peter said, we are "partakers of the divine nature" (2 Peter 1:4). This new nature enables the believers to live holy lives "according to the power that works in us" (Eph. 3:20).

Holiness is better understood when the word is seen with its companions. Holy, holiness, sanctify, sanctification, and saints in both Hebrew and Greek come from the same root word. Literally, the words at their root mean *separation to God*. The resultant state of being, intended by God for His people, is conduct becoming those separated. Holiness is a two-edged sword meaning separated from sin and separated unto God for His use.

To be holy means to be set apart for God's use. Sandy's instincts, fed by Bible truths learned as a youth and filed secretly away without use for years, caused her to make an immediate and complete break with her sinful environment. In order to be set *aside* for the Lord she had to be set *apart*.

Don't wait until you bang your nose into this plateglass realization to make your wholehearted commitment to holiness.

Positional sanctification is an act performed by God at the moment of salvation, whereby He sets the believer aside for His use. This is a once-and-for-all supernatural act. To be holy means to be set apart for God, partaking of a holy standing before God in Christ at the moment of salvation (1 Cor. 1:30).

Progressive sanctification is a process which goes on constantly throughout the believer's life in which God sets the believer apart for God's use in his experiences by eliminating sin and producing the fruit of righteousness.

The principles of positional and progressive sanctification often result in the imperfect amid the perfect. At the moment of salvation, the believer is perfect, "in Christ," though progressively often imperfect "in the world." This should not be and must not be rationalized, but any momentary relapse verifies it. Every aberrant act confirms the fact that we must progress.

As a college student majoring in horticulture I often was required to do grafting. Resulting was a plant with the characteristics of the scion inserted in the old root stock. A scion is a branch from another plant with characteristics desired from an unproductive root. One project required that I graft a camellia garden, using common root stock that by nature produced small, poorly formed blossoms. I grafted in the newly emerging beautiful "Dr. Tinsley" variety. The scions grew well, and in a few years produced beautiful flowers. Occasionally a malformed blossom would be found on a plant. When this happened it was necessary to check the root stock below the line where the scion had been inserted. Every time the bud had come from a shoot off of the old stock, it was always trimmed off.

No one could deny that the plant had produced such unappealing buds. However, they were not characteristic of or becoming to the new nature of the plants.

Spiritually our new nature is grafted into our old nature. Every unbecoming sin comes from the old root and must be pruned away. This perpetual pruning process is intended to let the characteristics of the new nature prevail. Thus, the plant is being set aside to produce characteristics becoming of Christ.

A holy person lives a life contentedly trying to make the positional and progressive more consistently one. This process begins and continues with a conscious effort, though it becomes increasingly reflexive.

Theologically, this initial, positive, faith response to Christ by a repentant sinner is called *justification*. It is God conferring righteousness on the respondent believer on account of Jesus Christ. At that moment the sinner is absolved from inherent unrighteousness, he is reconciled with God, his sins are forgiven, he is adopted as God's child only because of Christ's work. Justification is the crediting of the righteousness of Christ to the account of such a person at the moment of new birth.

Sanctification, by contrast with justification, always manifests itself in deeds of goodness, in the constant battle against sin, and in an ongoing endeavor to perform life in accordance with God's will. This process, which produces a holy life, is the progressive aspect of sanctification.

Scripture always shows sanctification to be the outcome of justification. Justification is the root, sanctification the fruit.

In 1580 the followers of Martin Luther drew up the "Formular for Concord" in which it was noted, "When a person is justified, he is also renewed and sanctified by the Holy Spirit, from which renewal and sanctification, the fruits of good works, must then follow."

This results in a life-style with the obligation and opportunity of living a holy life; one evidently being used in a manner pleasing to God (1 Pet. 1:15-16).

Hearing from Sandy some years after her new birth it was obvious that as the clock had not stood still for her, neither had she remained static for Christ. She had progressed in her maturity in the Word and service in the world. Through Bible study she had ingested God's Word. By ministering in and through her church, she had made it evident that she had also digested it.

We must each become aggressive and expressive or we become regressive and depressive. The sooner you get your arms around this truth the happier you will be.

John aids this holy hug by advocating three exercises. These are to be reviewed in the spirit of Paul's appeal: "Examine yourselves as to whether you are in the faith. Prove yourself" (2 Cor. 13:5).

First, one who is growing in holiness . . .

AVOIDS THE PRACTICE OF SIN

John said, "These things I write to you, that you may not sin" (1 John 2:1).

This truth in light of Christian practice has left some skeptics scoffing and mocking. His recording of "these things" is an aid assisting Christians to avoid sinning. "That you may not sin." He did not imply any "would not sin." Sin is always wrong and never right. A constant vigil must be maintained against sin, and a perpetual attention given to holiness. However, not only does experience evidence that Christians do sin, but persons who think this verse teaches they *do not* sin fail to read the entire verse. It goes on to state, "And if anyone sins, we have an Advocate with the Father, Jesus Christ the righteous." If it were not apparent that Christians sin, though they should not, why would they need an advocate, a defense attorney? The "if" selected for use by the inspired penman means "if, and they will."

This principle of a believer needing to be cleansed time and again after salvation is also stressed in 1 John 1:9: "If we confess our sins, he is faithful and just to forgive our sins and to cleanse us from all unrighteousness."

With laughter, cynics claim a conflict with this truth and one stated in 1 John 3:6: "Whoever abides in Him does not sin . . ."

First John 1:9 and 1 John 3:6 are reconciled by a bridge formed by 1 John 2:1-2. These things are written "that you may not sin." That is, they are intended to be (a) an encouragement to avoid sin, and (b) to let it be known that it is possible to avoid any sin. That possibility exists because He provides a way of escape. The only reason it is not a reality is that believers often fail to take the way out. In these instances when sin, which is out of character, is committed, we can be cleansed.

A close look at the verbs used in 1 John 3:6-10 enables this to be better understood. This complex grammatical explanation is essential to understanding. The verbs are linear active indicative tense, meaning constant and compulsive action. It simply means a Christian *does not willfully, habitually practice sin,* a sinful life-style is not maintained. It does not mean a Christian is sinless, but it does mean he or she sins less, and that sin is never deliberate and is always an exception.

The mind of a critic familiar with the Scripture might scroll through verses and quizzically settle on those using the word "perfect" related to believers. The Greek word for "perfect," *teleios,* signifies having reached its intended end, complete, or finished. No allusion to spiritual perfection is contained in the word. Rather it means grown or mature.

To complete a house is to "perfect" it, that is finish it. That does not mean the house is flawless. For a person physically to be "perfect" means he or she is mature, not that he or she is without any physical limitations or flaws. Though the word does not imply sinless perfection, we should not diminish its appeal to strive for holiness.

A definite, specific act is the reference of the Greek verb used in 1 John 2:1-2. Thus, incidents of sin, such as in the lives of Abraham, Moses, and Peter, may occur; but they are exceptions and not the norm or standard for their lives.

All sin is forgivable, but none is excusable.

Christ breaks the chains that bind a believer to habitual, compulsive sin. He is committed to and capable of doing so. Therefore, when a believer sins, full responsibility must be taken by the individual for the act. It represents a moment when the individual failed to take advantage of spiritual resources.

Second, one who is growing in holiness . . .

ACCEPTS THE PURPOSE
OF SANCTIFICATION

When a person receives Christ a new nature is imparted. This is called regeneration. In conversation with Nicodemus, Christ referred to it as being "born again." This second-time birth is into the family of God. *Re* means "again," and *generation* means "birth."

> Regeneration gives us a new PARENT, nature.
>
> Justification gives us a new POSTURE, standing.
>
> Sanctification gives us a new POSITION, set apart.
>
> Glorification gives us a new PLACEMENT, heaven.

In the same passage in which John exhorts us to holiness he explains how it is possible. In reference to Christ's relationship with a believer he says, "His seed remains in him" (1 John 3:9). "Seed" translates the Greek *sperma*. In natural birth, the characteristics of the nature of the father are transmitted in this manner, that is, by the sperm. In spiritual birth, God's nature is implanted in us, transmitted to us, by the Father. New nature results and remains. The character of the Father "remains in him." This is what enables the believer to become an overcomer.

God-like spiritual resources within the believer make possible the victorious, holy life-style. Triumph is found in the new nature. "Nature" means disposition or temperament. Combat between the old and the new is lifelong. When the old prevails, sin ensues. When the new nature controls, a holy life-style is enabled. This is what He has sanctified, set us aside for. If He has set you aside for a purpose, that means your life has purpose. Every person who says his life is without purpose has missed this point. He has set us aside in order that day by day He might mold us more nearly into the image of Christ. This emerging image has two purposes. First, it brings fulfillment and joy to the one being molded. Second, it becomes a living demonstration to others of the power of God to transform lives. Such a life becomes a living advertisement of the power and purpose of God.

"I don't see why God made me," moaned a depressed teenager. "He didn't," answered her pastor, "He is still working on you." Creatively, He is consistently trying to construct us into the image He has in mind for us to be. His nature is constantly being absorbed into different aspects of our lives. He is never finished with us. This is our hope, the only antidote for sin in our life.

"Two verbs," Augustine said, "have built two

empires—the verb *to have* and the verb *to be*." An empire built by the verb *to have* is a kingdom of things, such as material possessions and power. The empire built on the verb *to be* is a kingdom of character, that is, Christlike qualities. Within individuals, between persons, and in international relationships these kingdoms constantly clash. This ageless conflict still goes on as each seeks to subdue the other. Only when *to be* wins the warfare is there peace in the heart. Though the battle never ends, more and more skirmishes can and should be won as God's character matures in a believer.

As an emerging evangelist, D. L. Moody heard Henry Varley say, "The world has yet to see what God will do with one man who will fully surrender to Him." Moody resolved, "By God's grace, I'll be that man!" That should be the self-assumed challenge of every believer.

Christ's investment in you is intended to pay great spiritual dividends. Even a great treasure improperly invested does not live up to its potential. King Tutankhamen lived about the time of Moses, but his enormous wealth was buried with him. Centuries lapsed before it was unearthed. It has been calculated that if it had been invested at only three percent it would have been worth three trillion dollars at the time his tomb was uncovered! However, during all that time its value was lost. That monetary equivalent is found in the spiritual life of many. Never let His treasured investment in you fail to pay dividends.

Third, one who is growing in holiness . . .

ABIDES BY THE PRINCIPLES
OF SCRIPTURE

Conduct moves relentlessly in the direction of its dominant imagery. Its mental pictures are its pillar of cloud and pillar of fire. For this reason the Scripture must be kept on the design board of our lives.

In his drive for holiness John appeals, "And everyone who has this hope in Him purifies himself . . ." (John 3:3).

"Purifies" is such a tense as to mean "keeps on purifying himself." Here is a question in part answered by John in his Gospel: "Sanctify them by Your truth. Your word is truth" (John 17:17).

In conversation with the author/philosopher/humorist Zig Ziglar he commented, "I have no difficulty believing that the God who created this universe couldn't find a way to author a perfect Bible." That is exactly what God the Creator did. The Holy Father who wants to make you holy has authored a Holy Bible. God's intent for this divine Book is that it might be a manual of holiness.

Bible study is a failure and a waste of time unless it makes us holy. Interpretation must be accompanied by application. Scripture is not intended simply to answer our intellectual curiosities about things spiritual. God alone can make us holy. He had chosen to do it in accordance with His Word. His Word apart from Him cannot achieve its intended end. That is why many who know the words of the Man without knowing the Man of the Word are critics and skeptics. Those who know both are on the road to holiness.

The late S. D. Gordon fondly told the story of an elderly Christian lady. As a lifelong student of the Scripture she had memorized much of it. Her wonderful memory faded with age. One verse lingered after time had eroded all others. She repeated it often, "I know whom I have believed, and am persuaded that He is able to keep that which I have committed unto Him against that day." Eventually, most of this verse was lost from her recall until there remained only, "that which I have committed unto Him" Her enfeebling last days resulted in even further mental deterioration.

In her last hours her lips were seen to be moving. Friends crowded near to hear if she were asking for something. Each time they heard her repeating one word over and over: "Him—Him—Him." In concluding the story Dr. Gordon said, "She had lost all the Bible but one word, but in that one word she had all the Bible." That one word in full explained her life of holiness in both her productive years and in her parting hour.

In the process of purifying ourselves there are some spiritual actions equivalent to those associated with our physical life.

Our physical self needs food, and so does our new nature. For this reason, Christ instructs us, "Man shall not live by bread alone, but by every word that proceedeth out of the mouth of God" (Matt. 4:4). We must feed upon His word to grow spiritually.

Our physical self needs cleansing, and so does our new nature. If it were not possible for a Christian to sin, 1 John 1:9 would not have been included in the Bible: "If we confess our sins, He is faithful and just to forgive us our sins, and to cleanse us from all unrighteousness." The prefix "un" means negative or minus righteousness and is a reference to the sins of a Christian. When a believer sins he or she should immediately name the sin to God and, agreeing with Him about it as being a sin, turn from it and ask His forgiveness. This confession results in cleansing.

Our physical self needs exercise, and so does our new nature. We are exhorted to ". . . exercise yourself rather to godliness" (2 Tim. 4:7).

The Hebrew word for "known" is generally used as a verb, meaning something you do. Thus, to know something meant to do it. In light of this, to know God's Word means to do it.

Dietrich Bonhoeffer, who was executed in a German POW camp one week before the camp was liberated, wrote in *The Cost of Discipleship:* "Only he who believes is obedient, only he who is obedient believes . . . You can only know and think about it by actually doing it."

Paul's secular contemporary, the stoic Seneca, wrote of a habit which, if we apply spiritually, will aid our growth in holiness,

When the day was over and Sextius had gone to his night's rest, he used to ask his mind: "What bad habit of yours have you cured today? What vice have you resisted? In what respect are you better?" Anger will cease and will be more moderate, when it knows it must daily face the judge. Could anything be more beautiful than this habit of examining the whole day? What a sleep is that which follows self-scrutiny! How calm, how deep and free, when the mind is either praised or admonished, when it has looked into itself, and like a secret censor, makes a report upon its own moral state. I avail myself of this power, and daily try my own case.

If we daily try our case using Scripture as the standard we will not end as did the Frenchman Papillon. Living out his life sentence on Devil's Island he had a recurring nightmare. Frequently, he dreamed he stood before a tribunal which shouted, "You are charged with a wasted life. How do you plead?" In his dream he would answer, "Guilty, I plead guilty!"

The way to avoid such a guilty plea is to resolve in the spirit of Moody to be God's holy person. A set-apart life is never a squandered life.

Four daily, repeated steps lead to and result in a holy life, that is, one set apart for the Lord's use.

First, there must be a deep conviction that you need holiness. Just as there was an initial awareness of the need of salvation before it was received, so there must be an awareness of a need to be set apart to live a Christ-oriented life-style.

Second, there must be a complete surrender to the Lord of all appetites, aspirations, and ambitions. Envision there being an altar of consecration on which each is willfully placed individually. This should be accompanied by a Gethsemane prayer of "Thy will be done."

Third, yield to the work of the Holy Spirit, Christ's Spirit in you, as a refining fire to consume all inordinate pride, lust, passion, and greed. Ask for cleansing that will leave you as pure as an unfallen Adam or Eve.

Fourth, fix your mind on Christ and seek always and only to please Him in everything while relating to all persons in love. As you work at perfecting your spiritual walk also polish your social graces in order to insure that if anyone is offended it is not because of your personality but because of truth with which they are in conflict.

A commitment to holiness needs daily renewal. Every Christian would be wise to engage in such renewed commitment on a regular basis. Such renewal enables a perpetual freshness in the Christian life.

At the time of her coronation as Queen of England, Victoria also became Empress of India. The Indian province of Punjab then became part of her Empire. A youthful prince ruled in Punjab at the time. His love for Queen Victoria resulted in him sending her a very special gift. It was one of the largest, rarest, and most valuable diamonds, the Kohinoor diamond. Because of its value the Queen had the cherished gift placed in the Tower of London with other crown jewels. Those who saw it marveled over it.

Years later, the prince, now an adult, visited England and called on the Queen. After exchanging the appropriate greetings he asked, "Your Majesty, may I see the Kohinoor diamond?"

The request caused a bit of uneasiness. Some speculated that he wanted to request that it be returned. Immediately, the Queen ordered her guards to retrieve the diamond with all caution. Armed, the guards brought the diamond to Buckingham Palace and presented it to the Queen.

All present observed closely to see what would happen next. With great care the Queen presented it to the Prince of Punjab. With a respectful, Oriental bow he accepted it. Slowly he walked to the window holding the diamond he treasured. There he admiringly looked at it in the natural light. Returning to address the Queen he knelt at her feet with the sparkling stone still in his hands. With depth of emotion he spoke, "When I was a child I gave you this diamond. I was too young to know much of what I was doing." As he paused, all present thought he was about to ask that it be returned. He continued, "Now that I am a man, and knowing fully what I am doing, I want to give it to you again in the fullness of my strength, and with all my heart, affection, and gratitude."

Many who genuinely gave their hearts to Jesus Christ years ago did so lovingly with childish understanding. Now, in more mature years it would be wise to make a contemporary adult commitment. To grow in holiness such a self-giving is expedient.

8

God with Us in *Honor*

Growing up in the small Mississippi town of Osyka we looked for excitement in small and often simple things. I was blessed to be reared in a large pre-Civil War house that capped a hill. My childhood was during an era when trains were still very popular. The Illinois Central Railroad ran through our town. On that fast track streaked *The City of New Orleans*. This sleek new train was the rage when it began its runs. All work stopped, and folks gathered to see it if they knew far enough in advance when it was coming. Frustration resulted when it slipped by without an opportunity to marvel over it.

I had an advantage which my buddies soon found out about. Just about five miles above town was an old duck pond. A railroad bridge was built over part of it. In retrospect there must have been a geological fault that ran from that pond beneath our house. That is the only explanation I have for the fact that when *The City of New Orleans* crossed that bridge it caused a slight vibration which could be felt if you sat real still in a rocking chair in my upstairs room.

Knowing the approximate time when that sleek beauty should be coming, I would sit in that chair, and my buddies would gather around. When I felt the vibration we knew *The City of New Orleans* was on its way. We had about five minutes to get out on the front side of the hill and marvel as she sped by. What a thrill!

We felt special knowing how to tell when our dream train would be approaching. As a result we were always ready. We could read the signs and tell what was coming. Others were often caught off guard unless we let them know too.

Jesus Christ has said, "I will come again . . ."

As surely as He came to Bethlehem in the hills of Judah He will come to the Mount of Olives in Jerusalem.

The first time He came to die. Next time He will come to reign.

The first time He came to be crucified. Next time He will come to be crowned.

The first time He came in dishonor. Next time He will come in honor.

The first coming loses its full meaning apart from His next coming.

Rather than get absorbed in the important details of His coming, consider the fact of His coming and Who it actually is that is coming.

I. HIS MARQUEE

Just as a marquee notes "coming attractions," the Scripture has posted certain signs of His coming. These signs are to history what those rail vibrations were to my rocking chair. They let us know what was coming. The world can't feel them, so those of us who can are intended to let the world know what's ahead.

Prophecy occupies about one fourth of all Scripture. The second advent of Christ is dealt with 1,845 times in the Bible. It is a dominant theme in seventeen Old Testament books. Nearly half of the New Testament relates to it. Every chapter in 1 and 2 Thessalonians closes with a reference to His coming again. Twenty-three of the twenty-seven New Testament books mention this event.

Parallel lines of prophecy run through the Old Testament regarding Messiah. One depicts Him as a suffering Messiah, cut off for the sins of the people. The other reveals Him coming with a rod of iron and establishing His kingdom on earth so that He might rule on the throne of David in righteousness. His advent in Bethlehem marked the beginning of the fulfillment of the first line of prophecy. The second advent is yet to come but will as surely fulfill all prophecy concerning it as did the first.

A few tremors and one or two earthquakes that should alert us to His imminent advent are worth noting. In considering this keep in mind that it is always better to look for the Savior than for signs.

The time preceding His coming will be one when the abnormal is accepted as normal (Matt. 24:4-8). Ours is an era of inverted values. Few things have shock value, outstanding feats and individuals are greeted with a nominal "ho-hum" and the miraculous is discredited by the make-believe world of media. In a culture where freak is fashionable, sick is chic, and virtue a vice, the abnormal is considered normal.

Before His return things will be as they were in the days of Lot (Luke 17:26-29). Sodomy was an accepted practice in that day. Recently this aberrant sexual behavior was declared by a major psychological society not to be abnormal. Resultantly, the "closet door" has been opened, and an act that has been the antecedent of death for many cultures has proliferated. Some subcultures in America would be an embarrassment to the ancient city of Sodom.

Prior to the return of our Lord things will be as they were in the days of Noah (Matt. 24:37). They were giving and receiving in marriage in a crisis time. With fundamentals being eroded and foundations being destroyed they went right on without concern. Marriage and home life had lost their value. Ambivalence in the Christian community and encouragement by the world has done much to destroy family life. A recent census report revealed that fewer people are getting married; those who do get married are waiting longer; increasing numbers are opting to live alone; and more marriages are ending in divorce. Within a decade the ratio of divorced to married people has doubled, and the number of singles living together has tripled.

Demon activity is prophesied to increase before Christ's return (1 Tim. 4:1). Ours is a heyday for the "black arts" and those who practice them. In Zurich there are over 2,000 mediums. Many American cities boast as many. In the villages of Normandy more than 300 temples that specialize in spiritism operate. Nearly every village in Italy is said to have its occult specialist. Animism, the worship of evil spirits, has dramatically increased in America. So-called "primitive religions" are gaining in respectability. It is estimated there are over 1,000 covens of witches and warlocks in America. Occult activity has grown to the point that one warlock in California said, "The second coming has occurred, only Jesus Christ didn't show up—Satan did."

Skepticism is to increase as Christ's coming draws nearer (2 Pet. 3:3-4). Persons skilled in such sophisticated fields as paleontology and unlearned drop-outs alike are saying, "All things have always been as they are and always will be. He is not coming again." That in itself is a sign of His coming. Every person who denies His coming is a verification that He will come. Those who advocate this rationale indicate they believe that if God did create the universe He locked it into a system, closed it, hermetically sealed it, and let it go on its way. In effect they believe in a closed universe. They reason: nothing has changed; therefore, nothing can change; therefore, it is unreasonable to anticipate divine intervention.

Permissiveness is to proliferate before the heavens are to open for His return (2 Tim. 3:1-4). Mediocrity is the mandate of the moment. Anything goes under the banner of "Do Your Own Thing." Tolerance, indulgence, and leniency are marks of the acceptable.

The existence of a Jewish state in the nation of Israel affords three dramatic marquee readings regarding Christ's return to the land of His earthly pilgrimage.

Jesus warned the people of His day of the coming doom of Jerusalem. He pleaded with His followers to flee when they saw the city surrounded (Luke 21:20-21). Nearly thirty-four years later under the Emperor Nero, a Roman army led by Cestius approached, set up headquarters on Mt. Scopus, surrounded the city, and prepared for its siege. Jesus had warned of such, but there was no way out. Jerusalem was hopeless. Fulfillment of the prophecy was impossible. What Cestius did then still has historians puzzled. He "recalled his soldiers from the place, and by despairing of any expectation of taking it . . . he retired without any reason in the world," wrote historian Josephus.

It was then the Christians remembered Christ's warning to flee. They forsook the doomed city just in time to retreat to Pella in the Decapolis, beyond the Jordan. After their exodus the Roman army returned under the leadership of Titus and conquered Jerusalem. On that bleak day Israel died.

The Roman legions under the command of General Titus captured Jerusalem and occupied the land of the Jews in AD 70. In AD 135, Bar Chocheba, a false messiah, made a desperate attempt to rebuild those parts destroyed. He nearly succeeded, but Hadrian the emperor quelled the uprising. When the Roman army returned their slogan was, "Hierosolyma est perdita"—"Jerusalem is destroyed." Thus began the age of the Gentiles.

The Bible spoke of a nation being born in a day (Isa. 66:8). After the British troups drove the Turks out of a land known as Palestine the British/Zionist scientist-statesman, Chaim Weizmann, persuaded the British government to issue a statement favoring the establishment of a Jewish national homeland in Palestine. This was known as the Balfour Declaration. In America a petition signed by 413 prominent Christians and Jews, urging the establishment of a homeland for the Jews, was presented to President Woodrow Wilson. His response to this action served to encourage the British to act. On December 11, 1917, General Sir Edmund Allenby led his British Expeditionary Force through the streets of Jerusalem to accept the Turkish surrender and end 400 years of Ottoman Turkish rule.

This prelude led to the United Nations Assembly establishing the State of Israel on November 29, 1947. Thus, a nation was born "in a day."

A second sign in Israel of Christ's return was to be the end of the age of the Gentiles (Luke 21:24). From the destruction of Jerusalem, shortly after Christ's ascension, the land promised Abraham's seed had been under Gentile control.

In June of 1967, the small army of Israel, outnumbered 80 to 1, won a victory against the combined Arab armies. The entire West Bank of the Jordan River, Gaza, the Sinai Peninsula, the Golan Heights of Syria, and the beloved Jerusalem for the first time in over 1,800 years once again came under Jewish control.

June 7, 1967, Rabbi Goren, chief rabbi of the Israeli

Army, led a contingent of Israeli soldiers through the Eastern Gate of the old city. They moved swiftly to the "Wailing Wall" on Mount Moriah where King Solomon first built his temple over 3,000 years ago. The rabbi carried a chair in one hand and a shofar in the other. Customarily Jews have an empty chair at certain celebrations, symbolizing their anticipation of the return of the prophet Elijah. The shofar, a ram's horn, was blown to signify the end of certain fasts. Combined they symbolized that the fast of occupancy of the land had ended and that the seat of the heirs of the prophet was once more occupied. In that moment a 2,000-year-old prophecy was fulfilled; the age of the Gentiles was fulfilled.

A third sign relating to Israel pertained to their language. Prophetically it was said the children would teach their parents their language (Zeph. 3:9). Until the early twentieth century, Hebrew was a dead conversational language. With the establishment of a Jewish state an educational program emerged. In the public schools Hebrew was taught. In the afternoons after school children went home and taught their parents Hebrew. Today many languages can be heard on the streets of the Jewish cities of Israel. Immigration has brought together many tongues. Still the children go home in the afternoons and teach the parents Hebrew.

Over 100 years ago the king of Prussia, Frederick the Great, was having a discussion with his chaplain about the truth of the Bible. Frederick had become skeptical and unbelieving, principally because of the teachings of Voltaire. The king queried, "If your Bible is really from God, you should be able to demonstrate the fact simply. Give me the proof of the inspiration of the Bible in a word."

Replied the chaplain, "Your Majesty, it is possible for me to answer your request quite literally. I can give you the proof you asked for in a single word."

In astonishment the King of Prussia enquired, "What is this magic word that carries such a weight of proof?"

"Israel, your Majesty." Frederick sat in silence, his answer received.

What is happening in the fertile crescent today is underscoring the prophetic message of Christ who said: "Now when these things begin to happen, look up and lift up your heads, because your redemption draws near" (Luke 21:28).

We should live as Martin Luther said he did: "I live as though Jesus died yesterday, rose today, and is coming tomorrow."

The first vision in the Revelation relates to the second coming (Rev. 1:7-20). John, the penman, had a mind saturated with Old Testament knowledge. Therefore, he drew many symbols from it to illustrate certain great truths. In this revelation are seen three factors regarding His return: His majesty (Who He is), what His mission is, and what His message will be.

II. HIS MAJESTY

The thrill of the return is not simply that Emmanuel is going to be with us but that He is going to let us be with Him forever after. His next coming will literally be *God with us* bodily once again. John spared no effort to let us know Who this is that is coming again.

A. *He is the "Alpha and Omega."* These are the spelled-out, anglicized forms of the first and last letters of the Greek alphabet. They are used to describe His eternal nature. He is "the Beginning and the End." This expression describes Him as being the complete, perfect, and eternal revelation of God. He was and is God with us. He was involved in *Creation*, is now involved in *Continuation*, and ultimately will be in Consummation. He created all things, controls all things, and will consummate all things. He is the beginning and end of all things.

To today's reader this is a revelation of His eternal nature and is theologically edifying. It was intended to be much more to the early readers and should be to us today. To those Asian Christians about to suffer for their faith in Christ this was encouragement. The fact of Who we serve should inspire us to be loyal to the royal blood shed for us.

B. *He is "the Almighty."* This translates the Greek word *pantokrator* which is the equivalent of the Hebrew *El Shaddai*, meaning "the sufficient One." Centuries earlier God had revealed Himself to the aged Abraham as "the sufficient One" *(El Shaddai)*. The occasion was the promising of a child to Abraham and Sarah who were beyond child-bearing age. This was impossible for man, but not for "the sufficient One."

We who serve Him now should live mindful that He

who promises is able to fulfill His promises. This is an intended stimulus to faith.

This title as applied to Christ (Rev. 1:8) is the same one often ascribed to God the Father. In deciding to trust Christ, one must remember He is not an untried God. He has been tried, tested, and proven through all of history. In all He has revealed Himself as "the sufficient One." Never has the word "sufficient" been so insufficient to describe an object. When He gets through doing and providing, His capacity remains undiminished.

C. He is the Abiding One. It is significant that John depicts the Christ who will come in honor as standing "in the midst of seven lampstands." These lampstands are identified as the churches (1:20). Emmanuel, He Who said, "I will never leave you," is revealed to be right where He said He would be: "in the midst." Emmanuel Who said, "Where two or three are gathered together in My name I will be in their midst," is thus depicted as keeping His word once more.

Those who minister in His beloved name should be encouraged by John picturing Christ as having seven stars in His right hand. These stars are interpreted as being "the angels [or messengers] of the seven churches." A characteristic of a star is that it has no light of its own. Its glow is reflected light. A believer's radiance is to be a reflection of the Son.

The right hand signifies strength and security. All believers can take courage from His protective grace. The eternally sufficient One will securely keep His own.

To accept this academically is commendable. To let it determine our attitudes and actions is an expedient. One who believes this can live in faith and act with courage and confidence.

III. HIS MISSION

When Christ came first, He came to be judged. When He comes again He will come to judge. He Who will come in honor will come as the Just Judge of all ages. Each item used by John to describe Him adds significant insight to this role. In the Revelation (1:13-16) these traits are observed.

His power is revealed by the fact that He is "girded." Modern weightlifters wear a wide, heavy-leather belt around their waists for strength and support. Christ is not girded around the waist but rather the "chest." This was a distinction reserved for high priests. It is the believer's High Priest who will come in honor.

Keep in mind that John's head was swimming with Old Testament types, forms, metaphors, and symbols. Using this reservoir he describes a "golden band." Such spoke of His Deity which had already been attested to by the previous titles.

"His head" notes His wisdom to judge justly.

"His hair," which was "white like wool, as white as snow," connotes His mature judgmental skills.

"His eyes like a flame of fire" indicate His ability to see, that is, comprehend with all clarity. He is capable to judge because He sees every act and knows every heart.

"His feet were like brass." All the instruments in the

outer court of the Tabernacle were brass because they all had to do with judgment. The laver where the priests washed was brass, as was the altar where sacrificial fires burned; so were all other implements. As being sure-footed speaks of stability, having "feet of brass" speaks of Christ's sure judgment.

"His voice" makes clear and certain His pronounced judgment.

In Hebrews 4:14 reference is made to "a sharp two-edged sword." Traditionally when a magistrate walked through the streets a servant walked before him, carrying a sword which symbolized the authority and standard by which he judged. Hebrews speaks of the Bible as the sword, whereas the writer of the Revelation says the sword came "out of His mouth." Whether written or spoken His word is the authority by which He will ultimately judge. This should solicit submission to the authority of Scripture.

"His countenance was like the sun shining in its strength." New Testament writers echoed the prophetic revelation of Isaiah regarding Messiah's disfigured face on which no one would want to look in His hour of agony. When He comes in honor and every eye shall see Him, His face will be radiant. His very bearing will indicate His satisfaction at having done all possible "to seek and to save." All efforts exhausted and all prophecy fulfilled He will come in His eternal brilliance to judge.

Lovely Venice was a city state ruled by a doge form of government for centuries. Their form of justice was swift and sure. The ornate "Bridge of Sighs" connects the

Ducal Palace with the New Prisons beyond the Rio. At one end of the bridge was the Avogaria, a series of rooms, in which numerous magistrates once presided. Here persons accused were put on trial. A limited, designated matter of hours was allotted for each trial. A massive wall clock showed the time lapse. Persons convicted were immediately led away over the "Bridge of Sighs" to be executed. The bridge was so named because prisoners were allowed to pause and view scenic Venice one last time before death. Many heaved a heavy sigh as they turned to meet their fate.

A unique twist of doge justice related to an accuser. If his accusations were proven false and there was no evidence to convict the one against which charges had been made, then the penalty that would have befallen the accused became that of the accuser.

Satan, the adversary who brings railing accusations against believers, can never gain a guilty verdict because we have our Advocate, Jesus Christ. Thus, our just punishment apart from the grace of God becomes that of our accuser, Satan. Ultimately the Just Judge will banish him to hell. Apart from the One coming in honor and glory that would be the destiny of each of us.

IV. HIS MESSAGE

In the last four verses concluding chapter 1 of the Revelation Christ's valedictory message is stated.

When John saw this awe-inspiring vision of the Christ who is to come he "fell at His feet as dead." Majesty deserves such honor. Integrity can respond in no other way. John's action was instantaneous bodily action that should typify our abiding, heartfelt humility before Him.

We, like the twenty-four elders, should cry . . . "You are worthy, O Lord, To receive glory and honor and power; For you created all things, And by Your will they exist and were created."

To us Christ's message to John has application. He said, "Do not be afraid." Literally, "Stop being afraid." Christ's peace which passes understanding was applied.

Christ said, "I have the keys of Hades and of Death." *Hades* in the New Testament is equivalent to *Sheol* in Hebrew in the Old Testament. Since the ascension of Christ it is a reference to the region of departed spirits of the lost. Hades is somewhat an anteroom, an intermediate state for the dead not in Christ, to *Gehenna,* the eternal state of the lost, the lake of fire.

This is a startling statement but true: hell is empty now. The beast and false prophet will be the first to go there. Next the devil will be banished there (Rev. 21:10). Then the unrepentant of all ages will exit the anteroom, Hades, and enter hell forever. It should be remembered Hades is no more pleasant than hell, and those who once enter there are certain of their ultimate destiny.

Isaiah (9:6) said ". . . the government shall be upon His shoulder." The keys are a symbol of authority, control, possession, and government. Christ is the ruler of the unseen world also. When a person goes beyond the day of grace and mercy in rejecting Christ, the key is turned. It is turned once and for all, forever and forever.

In hell there will be no infidels. All will be believers. Even those who have rejected Him in time will in their eternal state confess Him as *pantokrator*. Every knee will bow and every tongue confess that Christ is Lord.

Even those in hell.

"Hell?" remonstrates the skeptic. Yes, there is a hell awaiting those who reject God's summons to heaven. He will take no one to heaven with a hellish enough spirit to reject Christ. To admit such a spirit into heaven would be against the will of the rebellious sinner and counter to the mood of heaven. There is a hell for the same reason there is a trash deposit. If there is trash there must be a place for it. If there are persons who willfully reject Christ there must be a place for them. Heaven isn't it.

After the Civil War, the most plush riverboat to cruise the Mississippi River between Vicksburg and New Orleans was the *Robert E. Lee*. Other boats were as opulent, but the Lee was the favorite of the people. Every Wednesday afternoon she left port for New Orleans.

One Wednesday, as was the custom, thousands crowded the river's edge to see the idolized ship weigh anchor. As the imposing vessel turned her nose down the river, folks waved handkerchiefs and shouted "bon voyage" to friends and relatives on board. Passengers leaned over the gunwales and stood on the deck shouting farewells. As the old boat pulled away, rang her bells, and blew her whistles, black smoke billowed out her funnels. Wild and weird songs were sung by the dock crew that sent chills up people's backs and tears down their cheeks. As the palatial boat moved out of sight beyond the river's bend the city people got one last look. This was the last trip of the *Robert E. Lee.* About two o'clock telegrams began arriving from Waterproof and Rodney. The Lee had caught fire, had burned, and had sunk in a short time.

A few who survived told of what happened aboard the *Robert E. Lee* in those last minutes. About midnight the captain discovered the boat was on fire. Immediately he gave orders to the second clerk: "This boat is on fire, and I want you to run down in the saloon and down the corridors and rap at each stateroom, and cry, 'Get up; the boat's on fire!' This boat will burn up in the next few minutes, and while you are trying to save these folks remember you must save yourself." Dutifully the second clerk started on his run of desperation. He rushed into the saloon and along corridors rapping on stateroom doors and shouting, "Get up; the boat's on fire!" As he ran he continued to cry out his warning, "The boat's on fire!" Time did not allow for an explanation; he didn't have time to argue or entreat. His efforts to save others and himself hastened him on his route. His responsibility was to knock on every door possible and shout a warning.

Various responses resulted.

One group got very angry. They were indignant that a class boat like the Lee would allow such conduct. They assumed the clerk was drunk and voiced their complaints to one another through the thin walls separating the staterooms. In their rage many swore they would report such unnecessary and alarming conduct.

A second group was highly amused at their rude

awakening. They thought it to be a drunken practical joke. They were heard laughing until the flames swept through the corridors and gangways, cutting off their exits.

Another group heard the warning but waited to hear it again. Every stride of the young courier took him farther away from them, and they heard him less clearly. In only a few minutes they were swept to a fiery death, along with the amused and angered.

Still another group appeared not even to have heard the warning. They slept on to the moment of their sudden death. To the end they remained insensitive to the imminent danger. They opened their sleeping eyes in another world.

The last group is the one that reported these various reactions. They believed the second clerk's message and fled without their possessions to save their lives.

That historical account represents the various ways persons respond to the alarming news of an impending hell. Some get angry, some amused, some hesitant, and some indifferent. Thank God some respond to the message and are saved!

"Amen" stands out in the middle of Christ's exhortation. A basic meaning of the word is "true." Thus, Christ is underscoring for emphasis this great appeal. What John recorded is true. Our responses should be immediate and appropriate. We who know of His coming in honor to judge should warn others. Those warned should respond lovingly and receptively. They might well shout with the heavenly multitude: "Alleluia! Salvation and glory and honor and power to the Lord our God" (Rev. 19:1).

Again return with me to the days of my childhood in my little home town. Visit one of my favorite places with me, the blacksmith shop. The smith was my dad's friend. Because of their friendship he would let me play with his magnet when he wasn't too busy.

It was exciting to play around the emory wheel where there were always iron filings. By holding the magnet above the pile of filings they could be moved about on the table. At a certain height the power of the magnet did not have any effect on them. By bringing it ever so gently closer, the magnetic force field would cause the filings to stir around on the table. As the magnet grew closer the reaction of the filings became more dramatic. The closer it came the more they responded. Finally, when the magnet reached just the right height, the filings would jump up to meet it, completely under its control.

So it is with the coming of Christ. As His coming draws nearer we should respond more positively to His influence. Soon we too shall be caught up to meet Him in the air.

Of all the glories ever seen there is one yet to surpass all others. "Behold, He is coming with clouds."

In amazement the apostles watched Christ ascend in the clouds. Just as He was seen taken away He is coming in like manner.

In that moment all earth dwellers can join the multitude of angels in saying: "Blessing and honor and glory

and power Be to Him who sits on the throne, And to the
Lamb, forever and ever!" (Rev. 5:13).

Every eye shall see Him.

The best news the world ever heard came from a
graveyard right outside Jerusalem.

The best news yet to be heard will be a shout from a
cloud that will be heard in the bottom of every grave!

Don't you just love cloudy days?

The doors of the Father's House,
Heaven's Doors,
And Earth's prison gates were opened that night.
Heaven's music accompanied earth's new Light.
Emmanuel came with us to be
And from pale terror to set us free.

"Therefore the Lord Himself will give you a sign:
Behold, the virgin shall conceive and bear a Son,
and shall call His name Emmanuel."

Isaiah 6:14
circa 754 BC

Can you fathom the mystery of the Almighty?
Can you plumb the depth of His Deity?
No!
But He can enable you to scale the
heights of your humanity.
Note clearly the footnote written on
every page of your life:
"God Reigns."

History is the whispering voice of God saying
"Here I Am!"
The page of history on which is written
the events of the resurrection morning
is God's Legacy of Love.
No stone of Pilate could restrain the Rock of Ages.
The resurrected Christ is
the Conqueror of death,
the Lord of life,
and the Victor over the grave.
He lives that you may never die . . . and
while living might have Abundant Life.

God's intended end for us is not
health and/or happiness but holiness.
Christ didn't come just to save us
from hell and for heaven but that we might be
on earth holy.
Holiness is loving God more than the things
He gives us.
A holy life is the most powerful influence on earth
because it is a transferral of the power of God.

Jesus in Bethlehem was God away from Home.
His presence is irrefutable evidence that
God loves you.
He came to cleanse the
barren badlands of your soul.
He came to let His joy flow through the
the spiritually arid regions of your life.
He, Emmanuel, "God with us," is here to
domicile in your heart.

One of the few inevitables of life
is that prophecy will inexorably
be fulfilled.
The prophet's role has always been
to discern "the signs" and unveil
the future as though it is history.
Uncompromisingly
a prophet is to declare His judgments
are sure.

"This same Jesus shall come again. . ."

Not even the iron virtue of courage
can sustain us in the Valley of the Shadow.
The most obdurate waver when facing
thought-paralyzing fear.
A ship at anchor in the harbor enjoys safe mooring,
but
is that all for which a ship is built?
The fatherland of hope is in the Father's hand.
Therefore, grant, Oh Lord, that I may not see
obstacles as an offense but as an occasion for obedience.
May my sorrows be exercises in
faith,
patience,
and hope.